REMEMBERING
GEORGETOWN

A History

OF THE LOST PORT CITY

DAVID MOULD & MISSY LOEWE

THE
History
PRESS

Published by The History Press
Charleston, SC 29403
www.historypress.net

Copyright © 2009 by David Mould and Missy Loewe
All rights reserved

First published 2009
Second printing 2012
Third printing 2013
Fourth printing 2015

Front cover, top: Johnson and Ward, 1862. Courtesy Library of Congress, Geography and Map Division.
Front cover, bottom: E. Sachse & Co., Baltimore, 1855.
Back cover, top to bottom: A postcard from the early 1920s published by B.S. Reynolds Co.,
Washington, D.C.; *National Photo Company Collection (reproduction number 30742), Courtesy Library*
of Congress, Prints and Photographs Division; Engraving by C. Bohn, circa 1800. *Courtesy Library*
of Congress.

Manufactured in the United States

ISBN 978.1.59629.681.7

Library of Congress Cataloging-in-Publication Data

Mould, David
Remembering Georgetown : a history of the lost port city / David Mould and Missy
Loewe.
p. cm.
Includes bibliographical references and index.
ISBN 978-1-59629-681-7
1. Georgetown (Washington, D.C.)--History. 2. Port cities--United States--Case studies.
3. Georgetown (Washington, D.C.)--Economic conditions. 4. Georgetown (Washington,
D.C.)--Social conditions. 5. Social change--Washington (D.C.)--History. 6. Economic
development--Washington (D.C.)--History. 7. Washington (D.C.)--History. 8. Washington
(D.C.)--Economic conditions. 9. Washington (D.C.)--Social conditions. I. Mould, David H.
(David Harley), 1949- II. Title.
F202.G3L64 2009
975.3--dc22
2009037767

Notice: The information in this book is true and complete to the best of our knowledge. It
is offered without guarantee on the part of the author or The History Press. The author
and The History Press disclaim all liability in connection with the use of this book.

CONTENTS

FOREWORD

I have always been impressed and a little envious of how effusive and protective Georgetowners have been of their incredibly rich and diverse history. Established over 250 years ago, this community has long endeavored to preserve its history through both the written word and the preservation of its historic structures.

The Reverend Thomas Bloomer Balch knew Georgetown was a special place when he presented a two-part lecture about Georgetown in 1859. Published that year in pamphlet form under the title *Reminiscences of Georgetown, D.C.*, Reverend Balch predicted that interest in Georgetown's history would increase "as the wheel of Time shall disperse more of its moss over these dwellings."

A generation later, lawyer Richard P. Jackson penned *The Chronicles of Georgetown, D.C.: From 1751 to 1878*, an incredibly detailed and fascinating social history covering the community's first 127 years. Jackson proclaimed on the book's title page, "I loved her from my boyhood—she to me was as a fairy city of the heart."

The century closed with the publication in 1899 of Sally Somervell Mackall's *Early Days of Washington*. Despite its title, the majority of the work is devoted to stories of "old times and old things" in Georgetown. Miss Mackall asked her readers to allow her to "unravel the golden thread that binds and holds in poetic indistinctness all that our people were doing in days long ago."

The celebration of the 200th anniversary of the birth of George Washington in 1932 launched a nationwide craze for all things colonial American and with it an increased interest in the history of Georgetown as an eighteenth-century river port. The following year saw the dual publication of *A Portrait of Old George Town* by fifth-generation Georgetowner Grace Dunlop Ecker and *Old George Town on the Potomac* by resident Dr. Henry Ridgely Evans. The latter was the first scholarly treatment of Georgetown's history, featuring footnotes and an extensive bibliography.

Thirty-five years would pass before resident Mary Mitchell added to the Georgetown canon with the equally erudite *Divided Town: Georgetown, D.C. During the Civil War* (1968) and its sequel, *Chronicles of Georgetown Life: 1865– 1900* (1986). In between publication of these two indispensable studies of Georgetown life in the second half of the nineteenth century, Mrs. Mitchell both wrote and took photographs for the armchair travel book *Glimpses of Georgetown Past and Present* (1983).

Last but not least was the 1993 publication of the landmark *Black Georgetown Remembered: A History of its Black Community from the Founding of "The Town of George" in 1751 to the Present Day*, by Kathleen M. Lesko, Valerie Babb and Carroll R. Gibbs. This extraordinarily important study of the long-neglected history of the African American presence in Georgetown deserves to be much longer than its 184 pages.

All of these titles were but a small portion of the Georgetown history archives housed in the District of Columbia Public Library's Peabody Room, on the second floor of the Georgetown Branch Library at 3260 R Street, Northwest. When a devastating fire broke out at the library on April 30, 2007, the loss of nearly three hundred years of Georgetown history was narrowly avoided. Books, photographs, maps, artwork, newspapers and manuscript material were damaged. Funds will need to be raised to conserve many of these items. Had total devastation taken place, the informational and cultural loss, not only to Georgetown and Washington, D.C., but also to our nation, would have been incalculable.

When the Georgetown Branch Library and the newly redesigned Peabody Room reopens in December 2010, I will be adding to the collection this book that you hold in your hands. David Mould and Missy Loewe have ingeniously described Georgetown as Washington, D.C.'s first suburb, and as such, *Remembering Georgetown* retells many of this amazing community's stories, as well as adding new ones. Hopefully it will serve as the vanguard to forthcoming published works documenting the history of Georgetown as it enters the twenty-first century.

Jerry A. McCoy
Special Collections Librarian
Peabody Room
Georgetown, D.C.

PREFACE

Few famous neighborhoods in America can compare with the lively history, fascinating inhabitants and high style of Georgetown. Hugging a hillside along the Potomac River in Washington, D.C., the small enclave of classic colonial homes, almost hidden behind the clamor of fancy stores, popular nightspots and high-end restaurants, holds a treasury of tales that mirror the story of America.

From its beginnings more than a century before the Declaration of Independence, the community that became Georgetown has been the home of mysterious Indians, sturdy settlers, brash entrepreneurs, visionary statesmen, legendary artists and architects, eminent jurists, big-hearted philanthropists, crafty politicians, vile criminals, gracious hostesses, high-flying financiers, ruthless slave traders, roughhousing soldiers and sailors, benevolent religious leaders, innovative engineers, pioneering scientists and inventors and courageous captains of ships, armies and industry.

Their heroic, charming, odd and amusing stories have been preserved by history-minded residents, who faithfully recorded their personal recollections through the years. Josephine Davis Leary wrote *Backward Glances at Georgetown* in 1947 "to give the reader a cozy little feeling" about the "sleepy little village of creaking garden gates, tree-lined, cobble-stoned streets, pocket-sized shops and lethargic lines of transportation." Richard Plummer Jackson wrote his *Chronicles of Georgetown, D.C.*, "to snatch from oblivion what otherwise would be lost." Sally Somervell Mackall penned her *Early Days of Washington* because "very few are left to tell the tale." And Grace Dunlop Ecker preserved her lifetime of memories in *A Portrait of Old George Town* to "paint a picture of the kind of people who lived here."

We are grateful that these wonderful local writers gave us the means to go beyond the courthouse ledgers and other documents that normally supply the data for history books. We are particularly indebted to Special Collections Librarian Jerry McCoy, for his generosity of time, knowledge, guidance and good humor, while he also led the painstaking effort to restore priceless pieces of Georgetown history that were almost lost when fire tragically struck the D.C. Public Library's venerable Peabody Room.

We also thank the staff members of the Library of Congress Prints and Photographs Division for their years of cleaning, recording, researching, scanning and uploading historical photos; Stephen A. Goldman Historical Newspapers for providing quick, helpful newspaper articles; the staff members of the Washington School of Photography (Teresa, Kelly and Susannah) for their support and kindness; and Hannah Cassilly and the staff of The History Press for their stellar editing and solid support. Above all, we thank our families, Salam Dahbour and Lisa, David and Lesley Mould, whose patience, support, understanding and love made this project possible and worthwhile.

CAPTAINS AND INDIANS

Explorers and Early Inhabitants

Long before European explorers discovered the New World, the area that is now the Washington, D.C. neighborhood of Georgetown was a busy crossroads of commerce for Native American tribes living and trading around the Chesapeake Bay.

Archaeologists have found evidence that primitive people populated the area as far back as ten thousand years ago. Stone tools and other remnants indicate that early inhabitants had begun hunting, fishing, farming, living in villages and perhaps making war as early as five thousand years ago. By the time Europeans came in the early 1600s, more than forty Indian tribes, most from the Algonquin language family, were spread across the Chesapeake region.

The Indians lived off the abundant wildlife in the forests and waterways and cultivated crops in riverside villages. Their homes resembled rectangular huts with rounded roofs, and around the houses grew small patches of vegetables, including corn and squash. Some families also cultivated tobacco, which they smoked in ceremonies and used as medicine. The Indians traveled by canoe and traded with other tribes along the Potomac River. The name *Potomac* is similar to an Algonquin word for "trading place."

The prehistoric inhabitants' stone tools included arrowheads, knives, spear points, scrapers and drills. The remains of ancient stone quarries have been found in the area, including one in downtown Washington, where a creek once crossed Sixteenth Street near the White House. The early people also fashioned pottery from soapstone and clay. Archaeologists believe that other tribes came from far away to barter their goods for these locally made implements at a village where the Potomac River intersects with Rock Creek, the site of present-day Georgetown.[1]

The most powerful tribal group in the area were the Powhatans, who were allied with a number of smaller bands, according to the reports of Captain John Smith, founder of the first English settlement at Jamestown, Virginia. Shortly after establishing Jamestown in 1607, Smith began exploring the rivers and woodlands farther inland. In 1608, he took a shipload of fellow Virginians sailing up the Chesapeake Bay and into the Potomac River. He entered the Potomac on June 16 and reported it to be "navigable one hundred and fortie miles." Maps that Smith and his crew made of the area were remarkably accurate, although modern measurements put the navigable distance—between the river's mouth and the falls that hinder further ship traffic—at about 120 miles.

Despite the less-than-complete accuracy of his mileage measurements, Smith recorded vivid descriptions of the lush countryside he encountered on his journey up the Potomac. The dense forests that lined the river were teeming with wildlife, while the streams and marshlands writhed with abundant populations of fish, turtles and other creatures. He saw no other human beings for the first thirty miles of his trek, until the ship rounded a bend and Indians suddenly began swarming out of the woods and crowding along the riverbank.

The captain's journal notes the shocking sight when throngs of barely dressed Indians "to the number of three or foure thousand" emerged from the trees. Smith wrote that the "savages, so strongly paynted, grimed and disguised," spied the English ship and began "shouting, yelling and crying as so many spirits from hell could not have shewed more terrible."[2]

As shocked and amazed as the Jamestown explorers were at the sight of the gaudily painted and noisy Indians, the Native Americans were likely just as taken aback by the unworldly spectacle of a large ship with its billowing sails and oddly dressed crew. The Indians clearly were surprised when the Englishmen began firing their guns, which sent the terrified tribesmen scampering back into the undergrowth.

Historians doubt that John Smith's expedition ever landed at the point on the Potomac that later became Georgetown. But most agree that another Englishman, Captain Henry Fleete, was familiar with the site and, by 1631, was trading with the Indians there. Fleete, the adventurous son of a well-to-do British lawyer, first came to the New World in the early 1620s seeking his fortune and traveling extensively along the Potomac.

His log books describe the area of Little Falls, a boulder-strewn stretch of whitewater rapids on the Potomac that blocks further passage by large ships. Fleete also wrote extensively about the Potomac's confluence with Rock Creek, about three miles downstream from the falls. Long before it became Georgetown, the intersection of the two waterways was a thriving Indian community called Tohoga.

In his journal entry dated "Monday, the 25th of June" in 1631, Fleete gushed glowingly about the

> *town of Tohoga, where we came to anchor two leagues short of the falls...This place is without question the most pleasant in all the country and most convenient for habitation; the air temperate in summer and not violent in winter. The river aboundeth in all manner of fish, and for deer, buffalos, bears and turkeys, the woods do swarm with them and the soil is exceeding fertile.*[3]

Fleete began getting to know various Indian groups in hopes of striking up trading partnerships. He was doing a brisk business with several tribes, particularly in furs. On one of his trading excursions in 1623, Fleete and his crew were visiting a village of the Patawomeke (Potomac) tribe near present-day Washington when the town was raided by warriors of the rival Nacotchantk tribe, also known as the Anacostans, who lived nearby. The fierce Nacotchantks slaughtered a large number of Patawomekes and their English guests and made prisoners of those who survived the attack. Fleete was among those who escaped with their lives, and the Nacotchantks held him captive for about five years until colonial officials in Virginia reportedly paid a ransom for his release.

During his time as a prisoner, Fleete learned many of the Nacotchantk customs and became fluent in their language. After being freed, he decided to resume his career as a trader, using his newfound knowledge of the Indians and their ways to help broaden his business. He returned briefly to England, seeking investors for his scheme to launch a trading empire with the American Indians for such colonial commodities as beaver furs, which had become all the rage in British fashion.

For years, beaver fur and the felt made from beaver skins were favorite materials for high-quality hats in England and other parts of Europe, where headgear had become a stylish indicator of wealth and social position. The hats were so popular that Europe's beaver populations had been hunted and trapped to near extinction, making the pelts even more precious.

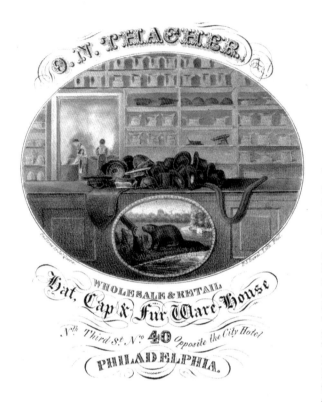

This advertisement from a fashion catalogue shows the enduring popularity of beaver fur hats, a fad going back to the late 1600s, when trappers and traders made a handsome living selling pelts from the American colonies to style-conscious customers in Europe and the New World. This ad was from the O.N. Thacher Wholesale and Retail Hat, Cap and Fur Ware House in Philadelphia in the 1800s. *Courtesy Library of Congress.*

The discovery of abundant supplies of beaver skins in America inspired traders such as Fleete to parlay their relationships with the Indians into fast fortunes.

Captain Fleete was savvy enough to know the value of publicity, and he persuaded a British journalist to publish a news story touting his proposed venture. The article, which displayed Fleete's clear talent for creative salesmanship, painted a vision of amazing riches to be had by trading with the Native Americans. The newsman wrote:

> *Fleete, newly come from Virginia, who having been lately ransomed from the Indians with whom he hath long lived til he hath left his own language, reporteth that he hath oftentimes been within sight of the South Seas, that he hath seen Indians besprinkle their paintings with powder of gold, and that he has likewise seen rare precious stones among them, and plenty of black fox, which of all others is the richest fur.*[4]

After rounding up a few generous benefactors in London, Fleete headed back across the ocean to start making money. He acquired a trading ship called the *Paramour* and hired a crew with funds invested by one of his English business partners, a merchant named William Clobbery. For several years, Fleete sailed the *Paramour* up and down the Potomac, visiting Indian villages and trading English goods for animal skins. Business was good, Fleete got rich and his British patrons made a handsome return on their investments. The success of Fleete and a handful of other ambitious traders inspired a rush of new fortune-seekers to trek across the Atlantic in search of new opportunity.[5]

When another large group of settlers arrived a few years later in the 1630s to establish the colony of Maryland, Fleete saw yet another business opportunity. He offered to act as a guide for Maryland's new governor, Leonard Calvert, who had been appointed the colony's first chief executive by his older brother, Cecil Calvert, who held the title of second Lord Baltimore. The Calverts' father, George, had been granted the land north of the Potomac—along with the title of first Lord Baltimore—in 1625 by King Charles I of England.

Fleete translated the Algonquin language into English when the governor first met with the Piscataway and Yoacomaco tribes in southern Maryland. With Fleete acting as an interpreter and mediator, Governor Calvert and the local Yoacomaco chief, called the *Werowance*, came to trust each other enough to make a deal. The Yoacomacos agreed to sell one of their riverside villages to Governor Calvert in exchange for the Englishmen agreeing to use their guns and other advanced weaponry to protect the Yoacomacos from their enemies. The settlers transformed the Indian village into St. Mary's City, which became the first capital of the new colony of Maryland.[6]

As a reward for his services, the Calverts granted Captain Fleete exclusive rights to trade with the Indians for beaver skins in Maryland. On one trading mission for Lord Baltimore, Fleet sailed a ship called the *Deborah*, which, its manifest showed, was loaded with a dazzling array of tools, trinkets, fabrics and other goods to be swapped for furs. The wares included seventy-four axes, twenty-six hoes, nineteen yards of Dutch cloth, sixteen pairs of Irish stockings, two yards of cloth called "peak" and a chest overflowing with beads, knives, combs, fishhooks, mirrors and small musical instruments known as jew's-harps. As his wealth increased and his local influence broadened, Fleete became a leading citizen of the new colony and later served terms in the legislatures of both Maryland and Virginia.[7]

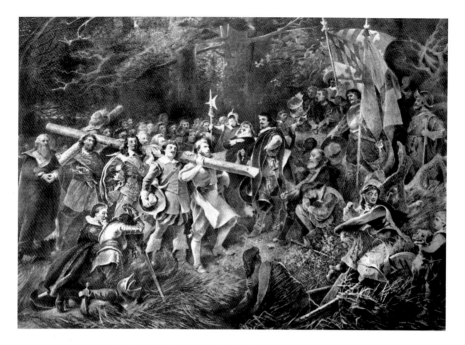

An engraving depicting Lord Baltimore's Catholic settlement in Maryland. *Photography by Harris and Ewing (reproduction number 22570). Courtesy Library of Congress, Prints and Photographs Division.*

Captain Fleete's industrious spirit and knack for knowing which colonial products would fetch handsome profits in England and Europe set the benchmark for success among Maryland's early settlers. Using Fleete's business model of procuring popular products from the wilderness and shipping them to eager buyers back home, entrepreneurs from the Old World found new riches in America, with merchants and planters becoming the ruling class of the emerging colonial economy.

THE SCOTTISH STAKE THEIR CLAIM

Establishing a New Colony

As the young colony of Maryland grew, more adventurers and entrepreneurs emigrated from Britain and European countries to make new lives in America. Maryland was particularly attractive to Roman Catholics, who were spurned in many other parts of the New World because of the Church of England's dominance in Virginia and other southern colonies and because of the stern Puritan influence in New England. Many groups that came to America to worship without persecution showed little tolerance for other faiths once they had established their own communities, which limited the choices for later-arriving religious sects.

Maryland's ruling Calvert family was Catholic, and, knowing firsthand about the difficulties of practicing their religion in Anglican-dominated England, they wanted to create a safe haven for members of their faith in the colonies. Maryland, therefore, became a refuge for Catholics in the New World. Under the system that governed England's royal colonies, the Lords Proprietors—with titles such as Lord Baltimore—were appointed by the king and had broad powers to make laws and land grants. Immigrants who were favored by the king and Lords Proprietors were given vast tracts that often became profitable plantations, making their owners fabulously wealthy. Early landowners frequently used their agricultural earnings to buy more acreage and expand their territories. Because of this trend, most of the area that became Greater Washington, D.C., was in the hands of fewer than twenty property owners by the early 1700s.

One of those early colonial land barons was a Scottish immigrant named Ninian Beall. A rough, red-haired soldier who stood at a towering six feet, seven inches, Beall (pronounced "Bell") had fought for King Charles II at the Battle of Dunbar when the forces of Oliver Cromwell invaded Scotland. The king's side lost, and Beall was taken prisoner and sent as a captive laborer to the British colony of Barbados in the Caribbean and, later, to Maryland as an indentured servant.

When he finished his service in Maryland, Beall was given fifty acres, which, through hard work, good business sense and bravery as an Indian fighter, he transformed into vast holdings along the Potomac River, including much of the area that became Washington and Georgetown. Around that time, land was being awarded as an incentive for bringing additional colonists to help populate the area, and Beall earned further acreage by recruiting new residents.

In 1703, records show that "Charles, Absolute Lord Proprietor of the Province of Maryland," granted Beall a 795-acre tract that included the confluence of Rock Creek and the Potomac River, site of the Indian village of Tohoga visited by Captain Henry Fleete about seventy years earlier. The Indian town was gone, displaced by the farming and population growth of colonial Maryland. With this acquisition, Beall now owned the property from the Potomac shoreline northward over a towering hill that afforded a commanding view of the countryside and the river winding toward the Chesapeake. Beall named a 408-acre parcel of his new property Rock of Dumbarton, after a famous geological feature of his Scottish homeland. He already owned an adjoining 225 acres on the eastern side of Rock Creek, which he had named Beall's Levels.

Throughout his career Beall, who achieved the military rank of colonel, held many notable and honorable offices in the colony. In 1699, the Maryland General Assembly passed an "Act of Gratitude" for his distinguished services in protecting fellow colonists from onslaughts by hostile Indians. Colonel Beall served as commander in chief of the provincial forces in Maryland. He was described as an imposing character and natural leader who had "a complexion characteristic of his nationality, with an unusually heavy growth of long red hair, and was over six feet in height, powerful in brawn and muscle and phenomenal in physical endurance."[8]

When he died in 1717, Beall had twelve children—six sons and six daughters. In his will, he distributed his property among his offspring, including his son George. The will read:

I do give and bequeath unto my son George, my plantation and tract of land called the Rock of Dumbarton, lying and being at Rock Creek, containing four hundred and eight acres, with all the stock thereon, both cattle and hogs, them and their increase, unto my said son, George, and unto his heirs forever. I do also give and bequeath, unto my said son, George Beall, his choice of one of my feather beds, bolster and pillow and other furniture thereunto belonging, with two cows and calves and half my sheep from off this plantation I now live on, unto him and his heirs forever.

The acreage inherited by George Beall, Ninian's eighth child, included one of two tracts of land that became the city of Georgetown, Maryland, and, later, the Georgetown neighborhood of Washington, D.C. The other landowner whose property contributed to Georgetown was merchant George Gordon, who, like Ninian Beall, came from Scotland. In addition to his landholdings and business interests, Gordon served for a time as sheriff of Frederick County, Maryland, and was a judge of the first county court. His contribution of land to Georgetown came from a three-hundred-acre estate he called Rock Creek Plantation.[9]

George Beall and George Gordon, along with a handful of other colonists living near the former Indian town of Tohoga, were enjoying solid success in their business ventures as Europe's demand for American products grew. Their tiny trading settlement, which a few years earlier had consisted of a few small cabins and a crude dock on the riverbank, quickly expanded into a busy seaport with wharves, warehouses, stores, houses and crowds of people.

Money by the Hogshead

The Tobacco Trade

The small Potomac seaport at Rock Creek was growing at an astonishing pace, fueled mainly by trade in tobacco. Of all the products the Chesapeake region shipped to England and Europe, tobacco was the most popular. Colonial planters were busy acquiring ever larger landholdings to expand their cultivation of the surprisingly profitable cash crop.

While earlier settlers such as Captain Henry Fleete got rich feeding the fashion fads of England and Europe, the old country's fancy for beaver hats had been eclipsed by a new fad—tobacco smoking. Explorers from a number of European nations had seen Native Americans puffing tobacco pipes and had introduced the fragrant plant to their countrymen when they returned home. Intrigued by the novelties of the New World, Europeans began trying tobacco and enjoying its effects. Pipe and cigar smoking became wildly popular across the continent. The most flavorful variety of tobacco was grown on the farms around the Chesapeake Bay and its adjoining rivers.

The colony of Virginia had discovered the market for tobacco after struggling for several years to find crops or other natural resources that would support its fledgling economy. With Europe's skyrocketing demand for Virginia tobacco, farmers who earlier had been worried about economic survival were now focused on keeping up with the mounting orders for their popular new product. The plantation owners were thirsty for additional land—to expand their profits and because nutrient-hungry tobacco plants would deplete the soil after just a few years, forcing farmers to move to new fields. Cultivation of the crop quickly spread from Virginia into the neighboring colonies of North Carolina and Maryland. Landowners around the Chesapeake and its tributaries who were not already growing tobacco swiftly switched to the new crop in hopes of joining the income bonanza.

In addition to the hefty profits for growing tobacco, there also was good money to be made processing the aromatic leaves and shipping them overseas. As the farthest inland point that oceangoing merchant ships could travel up the Potomac, which flowed through the center of the newest tobacco-growing region, the river port that became Georgetown suddenly found its docks besieged by farmers delivering large loads of tobacco to boats bound for Europe.

Warehouses and tobacco processing facilities sprang up along the town's waterfront, and the booming export business prompted other enterprises to arise around it. Makers of large wooden barrels called hogsheads, which were used as shipping containers for tobacco, set up shop near the warehouses. Each hogshead held about one thousand pounds of tobacco. The big barrels were hauled on wagons, rolled on their sides or pulled by horses. Long axles were inserted through the middle of a hogshead, allowing it to roll behind the horse like a giant wagon wheel. So many of the large round casks were being pulled into the town that streets leading to the docks were nicknamed "rolling roads."

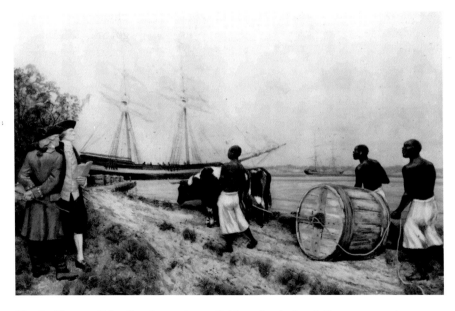

The "rolling road" leading from tobacco fields to the docks of Georgetown, where the big barrels called hogsheads were shipped overseas. Slave labor was a major factor in the success of the colonial tobacco business. *Courtesy Library of Congress, Prints and Photographs Division.*

Merchants and shippers whose wharves, warehouses and sailing vessels carried American tobacco to England and other European markets were making big money as the Old World's newfound love of smoking continued to soar. Any business that had anything to do with tobacco was prospering.

Among the most profitable tobacco-related enterprises was the slave trade. In addition to requiring vast amounts of new farmland, tobacco was extremely labor intensive. Cultivating and harvesting the crop was exhaustingly hard work that required a large number of field hands. Early tobacco growers were able to rely on indentured servants to grow and process their crops, but as demand grew and plantations became larger and more numerous, the shortage of low-skilled workmen was addressed by importing slaves from Africa or other colonies in the American South, where slave labor was being used to cultivate rice, another major colonial cash crop that grew in hotter climates, and from the Caribbean, where English colonists had been using slave labor on sugar cane plantations.

Slave traders established markets near the shipping centers around the Chesapeake, and soon the number of African workers, some purchased as slaves by plantation owners and some who came as indentured servants and eventually earned their freedom, rivaled the European population in Maryland and Virginia.

Because tobacco was by far the most valuable commodity in the Chesapeake colonies, it often replaced money as the local currency, and almost everyone in the region was growing some amount of tobacco. People were allowed to pay taxes and legal fines with tobacco, which the government could always sell for cash or trade for goods and services. One English writer called tobacco "the meat, drink, clothing and money of the colonists."[10]

Several varieties of tobacco were produced in the colonies, and a special type that grew particularly well along the banks of the Potomac and other nearby rivers was called "sweetscented" tobacco. Its rich, sugary flavor had the greatest appeal among sophisticated smokers in England and was, therefore, considered superior to varieties grown farther south in Virginia and North Carolina. Sweetscented tobacco was in such high favor that its sales became the dominant force in Maryland's economy. Richard Blome, a colonial-era commentator, wrote in 1672 that "the general trade of Maryland depends chiefly upon tobacco, which being esteemed better for a foreign market than that of Virginia, finds greater vent abroad."

The tobacco export business grew swiftly and steadily through the years. In 1622, England was importing about 60,000 pounds per year from the colonies. Five years later, the amount had jumped to 500,000 pounds per

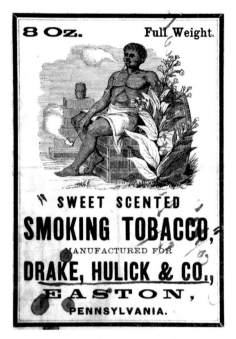

An advertisement from the 1800s for the sought-after "sweetscented" tobacco, an especially tasty variety grown on the Maryland shores of the Potomac and other nearby rivers. *Courtesy Library of Congress.*

year, and by the end of the 1640s, American farmers were selling 1.5 million pounds of tobacco annually to England. The trend continued, and by 1700, the British were buying more than 20 million pounds of American tobacco per year.

But tobacco was not a consistent ticket to prosperity. The crop suffered from a delicate life cycle and could be ruined by dry weather, too much rain, fungus and pesky parasites such as tobacco worms, which could quickly devour the large leaves. Tobacco also needed to be properly cured for good smoking and could be damaged if it became too moist or dry during the curing or shipping process. In addition, prices could fluctuate wildly depending on crop production, leaving farmers and shippers with occasional years of low profits or even losses.

One early description of difficulties facing the farmer of tobacco noted that "it neither supplied food to him nor fodder to his beasts; it could not yield him roof-timber nor firewood. He had to shelter, watch over, nurse it at every stage of growth and curing, for never was there a more tender plant or one subject to a greater variety of plagues, diseases and disasters."[11]

Because of the tobacco plant's sensitivity and the Mid-Atlantic region's unpredictable weather, some years produced bumper crops and some years were disasters. And when the growing season was too good, over-abundant production often meant over supplies that drove down prices.

Along with the highs and lows of production came quality issues. To make up for lost earnings when prices dropped, some less scrupulous farmers mixed lower-quality leaves and even floor sweepings into their tobacco to boost weight and volume. This practice made buyers wary of "trash tobacco" and prompted officials in Maryland to enact inspection rules to help guarantee quality.

Seeing another opportunity for tobacco-related profits, merchant George Gordon—one of the landowners whose property later became the city of Georgetown—decided to capitalize on the new quality-assurance laws. He built an official "inspection house" about 1740 to assess and approve shipments of sweetscented tobacco bound for England. Gordon located his facility on the banks of the Potomac next to Rock Creek, the same site that more than one hundred years earlier was the Indian fur-trading village of Tohoga. Gordon had bought the tract from another planter in 1734. The property, nicknamed "Knave's Disappointment," became part of Gordon's larger holdings in the area, called Rock Creek Plantation.

Despite occasional bad years for the tobacco trade, the intersection of Rock Creek and the Potomac River continued to be a busy trade port, with farm products and other goods arriving daily at its docks for shipment to the markets of Europe, the Caribbean and other American colonies. For several years, George Gordon's inspection house was the only tobacco quality-control station in the jurisdiction of Frederick County, Maryland, which guaranteed a steady flow of hogsheads to be officially approved before being loaded aboard ships bound for England. The inspection house also was called the "Rolling House" because of the steady stream of tobacco hogsheads that regularly were rolled into and out of the building after traveling into town on the "rolling roads." The tobacco inspection facility helped make Gordon one of the region's most successful businessmen.

THE GEORGES OF GEORGETOWN

"Knave's Disappointment"

George Gordon's tobacco inspection house and the other tobacco-exporting facilities at the Rock Creek port had transformed the once tiny settlement into an up-and-coming crossroads of global commerce. In the early 1750s, a number of colonial leaders decided it was time for the busy shipping hub to become an official city.

On May 15, 1751, the Assembly of the Province of Maryland authorized the laying out of a new municipality in Frederick County, which had been carved out of Prince Georges County in 1748, along the Potomac River near the mouth of Rock Creek. The legislators ordered a survey to determine boundaries for the city, which was to cover about sixty acres and be called George Town. While no definitive documentation has been found, some historians speculate that the town likely was named in honor of King George of England.

The survey was completed on February 28, 1752, and land covering parts of George Gordon's Rock Creek Plantation, including his "Knave's Disappointment" property, and George Beall's Rock of Dumbarton was determined to be the "most convenient" location for the new town. The city would be bounded by the Potomac River to the south and extended west to the present Georgetown University campus. The eastern border roughly followed the present-day Thirtieth Street, and the northern line ran a few feet south of the present-day N Street. The original lines were marked by boundary stones, one of which still can be found in the garden of a home at 3014 N Street.

The town was subdivided into eighty lots. The government informed Beall and Gordon that, in exchange for handing over their landholdings, each man could claim any two lots he desired. Gordon, perhaps seeing future business opportunities stemming from the incorporation, quickly agreed to the terms and chose his lots, numbers 48 and 52.

But George Beall was furious. Then in his sixties, Beall could not imagine that the prime property bequeathed to him by his famous father forty years earlier could be snatched away by a vote of some government body. He angrily decried the proposal and refused to recognize the legislative and legal proceedings aimed at confiscating land that was rightfully his. Local commissioners, appointed by the legislature to oversee formation of George Town, had little patience or sympathy for Beall and notified him that "if he did not make his choice of lots within 10 days from February 28th, he could only blame himself for the consequences."

After stewing over the situation for a week, Beall reluctantly relented and sent the commission a letter, which read:

> *If I must part with my property by force, I had better save a little than be totally demolished. Rather than none, I accept these lots, numbers 72 and 79, said to be Mr. Henderson's and Mr. Edmonston's. But I do hereby protest and declare that my acceptance of the said lots, which is by force, shall not debar me from future redress from the Commissions or others, if I can have the rights of a British subject. God save the King. GEORGE BEALL. March 7, 1752.*[12]

Beall and Gordon were paid for their land, in addition to receiving the lots.

Whatever official protests Beall might have lodged against the government's seizure of his inheritance to establish George Town, they were unsuccessful. But far from being "totally demolished," as his letter pessimistically predicted, Beall continued a brilliant career and remained a prominent fixture of business and society in the community.

The new city began organizing its governing structures, and because of its status as a key shipping port, it also became a significant center of commerce and culture. Historians attribute much of Georgetown's success to the nature of its founding families. Most came to the area for business reasons, in contrast to other colonial towns whose initial inhabitants were fleeing religious persecution or escaping debt or some other legal entanglement. With a prime location, a focus on business and a popular product to sell, Georgetown, Maryland, was on its way to becoming an economic powerhouse in colonial America.

Tycoons and Taverns

The Port City Prospers

Maryland's newest official city was a busy place, flourishing as a center for importing merchandise from Europe and the Caribbean and for exporting colonial goods, including flour, which became the region's second most important product when farmers discovered that fields "worn out" by tobacco cultivation were still abundantly fertile for wheat.

"Wharves were thronged with vessels sailing across the seas laden with the 'precious weed' and with wheat brought in from plantations for the 'flouring mills' in great Conestoga wagons painted red and blue drawn by six-horse teams adorned with gay harness and jingling bells," local historian Grace Dunlop Ecker wrote in her 1933 book *A Portrait of Old George Town*.

> *Also, there was a thriving coastwise trade, up to old Salem and Newburyport where the clipper ships were built, and down to the West Indies. These ships brought back sugar, molasses and rum, and from the Old Country came clothing, and furniture, and all sorts of luxuries, for the thriving merchants were building comfortable homes and furnishing them in elegance and taste.*[13]

During the time that George Town was coming into its own as a city, the American colonies became embroiled in the conflict known as the French and Indian War, when British subjects in England and its colonies were at odds with France, and French forces in America were allied with a number of Indian tribes. The French and British were fighting over control of land

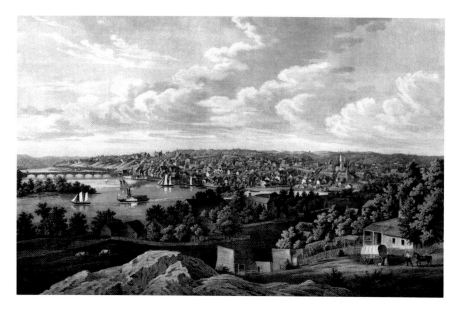

An engraving of ships approaching the Georgetown waterfront as viewed from a high ridge above the city. *Courtesy E. Sachse & Co., Baltimore, 1855.*

in the American interior, and soldiers involved in the engagements, including twenty-one-year-old Major George Washington of the military forces of neighboring Virginia, often passed through George Town, which, as the town continued to grow, was almost as often written as "Georgetown."

One such military contingent was led by British general Edward Braddock, who commanded Virginia colonial forces against the French in 1755. He landed his troops in Alexandria, Virginia, and marched them along the shores of the Potomac to where the ferry crossed to Georgetown. Braddock and a group of his men stayed briefly in the city before proceeding northward toward Pennsylvania and the famous Battle of Fort Duquesne, where Braddock was killed and his troops suffered a crushing defeat.

Braddock, a Scotsman who was welcomed warmly by the many Scottish families in Georgetown, wrote of the visit to a friend in England, saying, "Never have I attended a more complete banquet or met better dressed or better mannered people than I met on my arrival in George Town, which is named after our gracious Majesty."

General Braddock and his troops found Georgetown a good place to pause in their trek to the battlefield because of the accommodations offered by the town's numerous inns and taverns. If the docks and tobacco warehouses were the centers of George Town's economic vitality, then the focal points of its social and civic life were the taverns. Ms. Ecker's history of the city notes that

> *with ships arriving and departing and the land travel passing from North to South and back again, besides the country gentlemen coming to town to sell their crops and tend to other business, there was need for many taverns, and plenty of them there were in George Town.*[14]

In addition to being watering holes for the sailors, dockworkers, tobacco handlers and other laborers and professional types working along the waterfront, the taverns also provided meals and lodging and served as places to socialize and conduct business. They frequently served as meeting halls for the town's political and legal affairs, and as such, taverns figured significantly in Georgetown's early history. The oldest written records of a tavern in Georgetown describe an establishment owned by innkeeper Joseph Belt, who was granted a license by the newly created Frederick County Court in August 1751 "to keep a Public House of Entertainment at the Mouth of Rock Creek."

Joseph Belt's tavern became a popular and important gathering place. Local news accounts frequently mentioned Belt's place as the scene of major civic transactions, including an auction in 1752 of many of Georgetown's original eighty lots, which were carved from the land of George Beall and George Gordon. The *Maryland Gazette* newspaper, published in Annapolis, carried an announcement in its March 19 edition that

> *notice is hereby given that the Land appointed by Act of Assembly to be laid out into a town, by the name of Georgetown, adjacent to the warehouse at the Mouth of Rock Creek, in Frederick County, is accordingly laid out, and the lots will be sold the 4th Monday in March, being the 23 of the month at the House of Joseph Belt, living in the said Town in ten of the Clock before noon.*

Belt apparently made a good living for many years as a Georgetown tavern keeper. City records show that in 1760 he bought two of the most desirable lots in town at the southeast corner of Water Street (now Wisconsin Avenue) and Bridge Street (now M Street) and opened another tavern where real estate sales and other local deal making took place. The *Maryland Gazette*'s September 19, 1771 edition carried an advertisement for one of

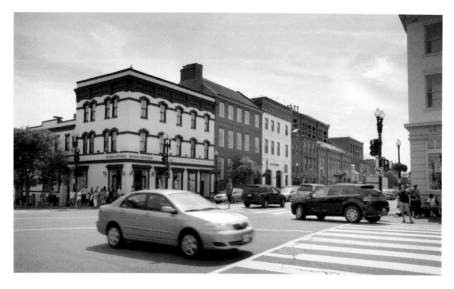

Belt's Tavern, an early focal point of business and society in Georgetown, stood at the corner of present-day Wisconsin and M Streets, still the main intersection of the community. *Photo by Missy Loewe.*

Belt's roadhouses. The ad, dated September 8 despite its publication in the September 19 issue of the paper, read:

> *The Subscriber continues to keep a House of Entertainment in George Town, at the Kings Arms, and as he is provided with Good Entertainment, Stabling, and Provender for Horses, would be obliged to all Gentlemen travelling and others for their customs and they may depend on kind usage, by their Most Humble Servant, JOSEPH BELT.*[15]

Another well-known tavern keeper was John Orme, who also operated a ferry across the Potomac to aid travel between Georgetown and the busy tobacco port of Alexandria, Virginia, a few miles downriver. In his petition for a business license, Orme promised "to keep Tavern in George Town, to keep good Rules and Orders and not suffer the loose and disorderly persons to Tipple, Game, or Commit other disorders or irregularities within his aforesaid House."

So much public business took place in taverns that their operators became de facto city officials. Townspeople depended on them for all sorts of services, as evidenced in a September 1760 *Maryland Gazette* advertisement for an upcoming horse race. Participants were instructed that contestants' names were "to be Entered the Day before Running, with Messrs. Joseph Belt and John Orme in George Town."

When John Orme died in 1772, his wife decided to continue the business and published a notice in the newspaper to tell neighbors and travelers that the place would remain open. But she was reluctant to continue her husband's trusting practice of extending credit to guests who preferred "running a tab" to paying cash. The ad advised that the "executrix" of Orme's estate "will continue to keep Tavern for ready money only.—Lucy Orme."

Dozens of other taverns operated in Georgetown, and several took on a "city hall" role, hosting regular meetings of local commissions, particularly a one-story wooden-frame establishment built by Joseph Belt at the northwest corner of present-day Thirty-first and K Streets and operated in the 1780s by a widely admired innkeeper named John Suter.

Suter's Tavern became the best-known meeting place in town and enjoyed a long and colorful history as a center of notable events in the development of Georgetown and Washington. Like so many residents of early Georgetown, John Suter was a Scotsman. Regular guests included George Washington, whose Mount Vernon estate was about fifteen miles downriver in Virginia. Washington lodged, dined and held numerous meetings at Suter's Tavern, including a famous session in which he signed the proclamation officially establishing the nation's capital on land just east of Georgetown. Suter operated the tavern until his death in 1794, when his son, John Suter Jr., took over.

Among the leading citizens of early Georgetown was tobacco exporter Robert Peter, who has been called the city's "pioneer business man" and a "merchant prince and land owner." Peter came to America when he was about twenty years old from the Scottish town of Crossbasket, near Glasgow. He first settled in Bladensburg, Maryland, before moving to George Town in 1752. Peter took an active interest in civic affairs and became Georgetown's first mayor when a reorganization of local government created the office in 1789. He worked as the American representative of a well-known shipping firm called John Glassford & Company of North Britain, Glasgow, which grew into one of Britain's most successful tobacco-trading empires. So much colonial tobacco moved through the port of Glasgow that merchants there became known as the "Virginia Dons." Another prominent tobacco tycoon was Peter's cousin, James Dunlop, who came to Georgetown from Garnkirke, near Glasgow, in 1783.[16]

In addition to Scotland-based traders, another giant in the tobacco business was the local Georgetown firm of Forrest, Stoddert and Murdock, formed in 1783. Partner Uriah Forrest, born in St. Mary's County, Maryland, in 1756, later served in the Revolutionary War, losing a leg in the Battle of Brandywine. He also was a delegate to the Continental Congress. His business partners were John Murdock, the son of an already established Georgetown businessman, and Benjamin Stoddert. Stoddert, born in Maryland in 1751, also was of Scottish ancestry and was the son of Captain Thomas Stoddert, who died with General Braddock in the French and Indian War. Benjamin Stoddert also fought in the American Revolution and became the first U.S. secretary of the navy.[17]

Georgetown's tobacco barons also included warehouse operators Francis Lowndes, John Laird and Henry Threlkeld, an Englishman whose thousand-acre estate along the Potomac called Berleith became the campus of Georgetown University. Another tobacco shipper, James Maccubbin Lingan, was the first person to hold the office of "collector" at the Georgetown port and, during the American Revolution, became a general in George Washington's army.

Other prominent citizens of colonial Georgetown were ferry owner Charles Beatty and shipper Ebenezer Dodge, who came from Salem, Massachusetts, and built a successful trade with the West Indies. His younger brother, Francis, also took up the tobacco-shipping business and became one of the richest people in town. The city's well-known lawyers

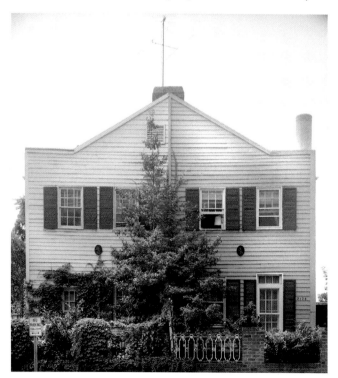

The early home of tobacco shipper Robert Peter, Georgetown's first mayor, at 3134–36 South Street. *George Eisenman, 1967. HABS (reproduction number HABS, DC, GEO,92-1). Courtesy Library of Congress, Prints and Photographs Division.*

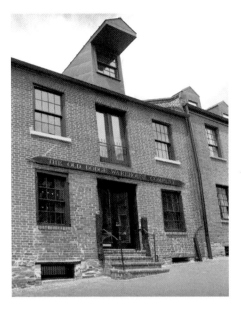

The Ebenezer Dodge Warehouse, once a prime shipping facility for tobacco and products to Europe and the Caribbean, has been converted to restaurant and retail space at 1000 Wisconsin Avenue. *Photo by Missy Loewe.*

at the time included Joseph Earle and Philip Barton Key, whose nephew, attorney and poet Francis Scott Key, later wrote America's national anthem.

Another local businessman who acquired substantial wealth in the 1700s was slave trader John Beattie, who supplied African workers for the labor-hungry tobacco plantations and other agricultural and industrial enterprises that needed field hands or servants. Beattie set up shop in 1760, with headquarters in the present-day 3200 block of O Street and auction facilities at other spots around town as well, including the Montgomery Tavern, located in the present-day 1300 block of Wisconsin Avenue.[18]

As Georgetown grew and prospered, slavery became a larger and more important factor in the region's commerce and way of life, with hundreds of African laborers toiling in the tobacco and wheat fields across the countryside and working as dock hands and household servants in town. As the tobacco economy expanded, slaves became an ever larger segment of the region's population.

The city's status as a major center of commerce made its merchants, planters and shippers increasingly wary of the new taxes being imposed on the American colonies by the government of Britain.

As tensions over "taxation without representation" intensified, a rising chorus of Georgetown businessmen began denouncing the heavy-handed regime of King George III. Leading townspeople were among the loudest voices at raucous tavern meetings, several attended by George Washington, to lend solidarity and support to other colonial ports such as Boston and Charleston, South Carolina, which were engaged in bitter disputes with the Crown's tax authorities. To protest the British Tea Act in 1774, several Georgetown merchants refused shipments of English tea and assisted in torching a tea-laden British ship in the harbor at Annapolis.

After the Declaration of Independence was signed, many Georgetown merchants and planters led campaigns to raise money, amass supplies, provide arms and recruit soldiers for the coming revolt. While no major Revolutionary battles occurred in or near Georgetown, many residents eagerly signed up for military duty, and several became well-known heroes of the War for Independence. One American military contingent formed in 1776 was commanded by George Beall's son Thomas, who achieved the rank of colonel, like his father and grandfather. The soldiers from Maryland earned a reputation for toughness in battle, prompting George Washington to speak admiringly of them as "the old line," which later gave Maryland its official nickname: the "Old Line State."[19]

The Revolutionary War years brought significant changes to Georgetown. The city's first post office, one of only seventy-five in America at the time, opened in 1776 under the management of Benjamin Franklin, who became the first U.S. postmaster general after the war. American postal rates were high in the 1770s, based on the number of miles a letter had to travel. Mail often took weeks to reach its destination, usually delivered by letter carriers on horseback. The cost of postage had to help cover the mailman's salary, his food and lodging along the route, the feeding and upkeep of his horses and administrative expenses. Rates could climb as high as thirty-five cents for a letter, an enormous sum in colonial times.[20]

In 1778, religion took on a stronger focus in Georgetown when an outspoken young clergyman named Stephen Bloomer Balch arrived in town and set about establishing the area's first congregation of Presbyterians, the traditional religion of Scotland, the ancestral homeland of so many residents. Balch's energetic spirit and personal popularity launched him on a fifty-year career of spiritual, civic and social leadership in Georgetown, bolstered by his marriage to George Beall's daughter, Elizabeth. Through the years, Balch was at the center of many of the most momentous events in the town's history.[21]

Balch arrived in Georgetown at a particularly difficult time. The Revolution was going badly for the American side, and the winter was one of the harshest in memory. Many men from Georgetown were among the troops struggling for survival with General Washington at the Continental army's snowy encampment at Valley Forge in Pennsylvania. The next winter, in 1779, was even more frigid, with the Potomac River and Chesapeake Bay icing over to the point that all shipping was forced to stop. It was so cold that horse-drawn wagons were driving over the frozen Potomac as if it were a roadway. Thomas Jefferson, in a commentary on the cold wave, observed that at Annapolis, Maryland, where the Chesapeake was five miles wide, the ice was five inches thick.[22]

The 1780s in Georgetown opened on a sad note with the March 15 death of original landowner George Beall at age eighty-five. Beall's son, Thomas, assumed many of the family business roles and began calling himself "Thomas Beall of George" to honor his father. When the Revolutionary War ended in 1783, Georgetown's land area doubled when a sixty-acre tract called Beall's Addition was annexed. The town got another twenty acres two years later when sixty-five lots called Peter, Beatty, Threlkeld and Deakin's Addition joined the incorporation. Still more acreage was added on December 25, 1789, with the name Beall's Second Addition.[23]

The town's growth and progress picked up considerably after the war when the new United States of America began to move forward as an independent nation. Over the next several years, dozens of new businesses materialized, including a leather works opened by merchant Thomas Corcoran in 1788 that gave rise to an economic dynasty that eventually placed the Corcorans among America's wealthiest families. The town's first bridge also was constructed in 1788, a span over Rock Creek connecting Georgetown with land to the east that later would become the city of Washington, D.C. In 1789, higher education came to town with the founding of Georgetown College by Roman Catholic clergymen.[24]

Georgetown's most famous frequent visitor, George Washington, received his most momentous welcome to the town in April 1789, when he passed through on his way from Mount Vernon to New York to take the oath of office as the nation's first president. The lead story in the *Times and Potowmack Packet* newspaper's April 23 edition reported:

> *Last Thursday passed through this town on his way to New York the most illustrious, the President of the United States of America, with Charles Thompson, Esq. Secretary, to Congress.*
>
> *His Excellency arrived at about 2 O'Clock on the bank of the Patowmack, escorted by a respectable corps of gentlemen from Alexandria where the George Town ferry boats, properly equipped, received his Excellency and suit, safely landed them, under the acclamation of a large crowd of their grateful fellow citizens—who beheld his Fabius, in the evening of his day, bid adieu to the peaceful retreat of Mount Vernon, in order to save his country once more from confusion and anarchy. From this place his Excellency was escorted by corps of gentlemen commanded by Col. Wm.*

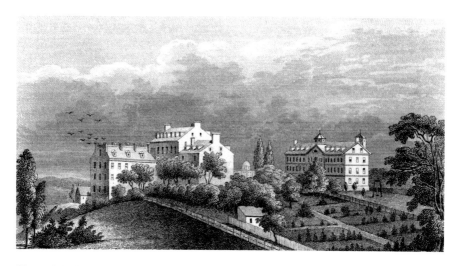

The early buildings of Georgetown College, begun in 1789 atop a hill on the western edge of the community. *Engraving by C. Bohn, circa 1800. Courtesy Library of Congress.*

Deakins, Junr., to Mr. Spurrier's Tavern, where the escort from Baltimore take charge of him.[25]

Washington's journey to New York was a highly celebrated affair, with delegations of local leaders meeting and escorting the presidential party along the way. Colonel William Deakins, a major landowner and shipper, was the justice of the peace, most likely Georgetown's highest municipal office at the time, and therefore had the honor of leading the presidential party through the city. Other members of the Georgetown delegation were former officers of the Revolutionary army, including Uriah Forrest, Benjamin Stoddert, James Maccubbin Lingan, William Beatty, William Murdock and Lloyd Beall, who had been adjutant of the staff of Alexander Hamilton and later became Georgetown's second mayor.[26]

After returning from his inauguration in New York, President Washington further elevated Georgetown's importance by putting the town on the "short list" of potential sites for the new nation's permanent capital.

The Capital Across the Creek

Building Washington

Georgetown's leaders waged a hard campaign to make their town the official seat of government for the United States of America. One of the earliest issues taken up by the first U.S. Congress in 1789 was the question of establishing a permanent national capital. Several cities were considered, and congressmen from the various states were pushing vigorously for their favorite locations.

During the years leading up to the Revolution, America's founding fathers had convened in several places, including Philadelphia, Lancaster and York in Pennsylvania; Baltimore and Annapolis in Maryland; Trenton, New Jersey; and New York City. It often had been difficult for delegates to the Continental Congress to find adequate accommodations, and it always had been a problem to move the ever larger volumes of records and files from town to town.

The U.S. Constitution, which was ratified in 1788, provided for a Federal District up to ten miles square (or one hundred square miles) as the territory for a capital, but there was no provision for a specific location. The question consumed countless hours of often contentious debate in the new Congress. The highly charged discussion finally narrowed the selection to two general areas. The first option would be somewhere along the Potomac River at least as far south as Georgetown, and the second possibility would be along the Delaware River above Trenton, New Jersey. Congressmen from the northern states favored the Delaware River site, while representatives from the South pressed for the Potomac location. The southerners, led by

Virginia's James Madison, argued that a capital on the Potomac would be closer to the country's geographic center.

Besides the question of where to establish the new capital, Congress faced the even thornier issue of how to pay for it. The Revolutionary War had plunged the young nation deeply into debt, and the huge amounts of funding needed to plan and build an entire city would be nearly impossible to find. Beyond financing such a project, there were also the questions of who would plan the streets, design and construct the buildings, build the infrastructure and supply the labor.

"The burning question before Congress at the time was a bill for funding of the public debt and the assumption of debts incurred by the States during the Revolutionary War, amounting to about $20 million," historian H. Paul Caemmerer wrote.

> *Alexander Hamilton, as the first Secretary of the Treasury, had recommended raising new money by issuing debt obligations of the United States government. His aim was to restore the value of the worthless continental dollar (a pound of tea sold for $90; a pair of shoes for $100; a barrel of flour for $1,500 in paper money) but, it was pointed out by several congressmen, that federal assumption of state debts would benefit northern states more than the agriculture states of the South.*
>
> *Thus we come to the famous compromise proposed by Hamilton about the middle of June 1790, when in consideration of locating the capital on the banks of the Potomac he hoped to secure enough votes to secure the enactment of the funding bill. Thus by the Act of July 16, 1790, it was definitely decided that the seat of government should be on the banks of the Potomac.*[27]

The action of Congress shifted the next decision to President Washington and his new administration to determine which site along the Potomac would be best suited for the new capital. Washington, a surveyor by training, was intimately familiar with the Potomac Valley, particularly the stretch from his Mount Vernon estate in Virginia to the tobacco port of Alexandria and onward to Georgetown.

Both Alexandria and Georgetown were in the running for the designation. Each would have benefited economically and in terms of prestige to be chosen, and leading citizens of both towns politicked mightily for the honor. Congressional records show that newly selected Georgetown mayor Robert Peter sent a letter to Congress on behalf of himself and his fellow residents, "offering to put themselves and their fortunes under the exclusive jurisdiction of Congress in case that town should be selected as the permanent seat of government."[28]

While Georgetown was given strong consideration, President Washington decided to create an entirely new capital city, outside of any existing town. But the winning site that Washington chose was just next door to Georgetown, on undeveloped land immediately across Rock Creek. Government surveyors laid out the ten-mile square called for in the Constitution in the shape of a diamond straddling the Potomac River, encompassing land from the states of Maryland and Virginia. Georgetown was near the center of the new territory, and Alexandria was barely within the boundaries at the bottom point.

The president made the selection of the new capital city's site official during a meeting held with great fanfare at one of his favorite Georgetown establishments, Suter's Tavern. Washington, Secretary of State Thomas Jefferson and other government officials convened in the tavern's dining room and wrote up a proclamation describing the location of the new city on the Maryland side of the Potomac. The proclamation's concluding lines read:

> *In testimony whereof I have caused the seal of the United States to be affixed by these present and sign the same with my hand. Done at Georgetown aforesaid the 30th day of March, in the year of our Lord, 1791, in the Independence of the United States the fifteenth. By the President, George Washington.*[29]

Jefferson also signed the proclamation.

With the location formally established, the president's next task was hiring someone to design the new city. That decision appears to have been far simpler than choosing the site. Even before Congress began the earliest stages of debate, French-born engineer Pierre Charles L'Enfant, who had served under Washington in the Revolution, began writing the president with ideas and suggestions for America's new capital. Once the proclamation was signed, Washington immediately hired L'Enfant, whom he knew and respected and who, according to most historical accounts, was practically begging for the job. "No better choice could have been made," historian Grace Dunlop Ecker believed. "L'Enfant applied his ability to the task with enthusiasm; the approbation of 'his General' gave him supreme satisfaction."[30]

Washington directed L'Enfant to set up a headquarters in Georgetown and begin working with a three-man commission, appointed by the president, and with a surveyor named Andrew Ellicott. When L'Enfant arrived in Georgetown on March 9, 1791, and checked into John Suter's Fountain Inn and Tavern, he carried a letter from Secretary of State Jefferson, who would be supervising the project on the government's behalf.

The letter told L'Enfant to

> *proceed to Georgetown where you will find Mr. Ellicott employed in making a survey and map of the Federal Territory. The special object of asking your aid is to have a drawing of the particular grounds most likely to be approved for the site of the Federal town and buildings.*

Jefferson also advised L'Enfant that "for necessary assistance and expense" he could "apply to the Mayor of Georgetown who is written to on the subject." The letter concluded by asking L'Enfant to file regular updates.

> *I will beg the favor of you to mark to me your progress about twice a week, say every Wednesday and Saturday evening, that I may be able in proper time to draw your attention to some other objects which I have not at this moment sufficient information to define.*[31]

L'Enfant's first report to Jefferson from Georgetown, dated Friday, March 11, 1791, indicated a slow start:

> *Sir: I have the honor of informing you of my arrival at this place, where I could not possibly reach before Wednesday last and very late in the evening, after having traveled part of the way on foot and part on horseback leaving the broken stage behind.*
>
> *On arriving I made it my first care to wait on the Mayor of the town in conformity with the direction which you gave me. He appeared to be much surprised and he assured me he had received no previous notice of my coming nor any injunction relating to the business I was sent upon. However next day—yesterday morning—he made me a kind offer of his assistance in procuring for me three or four men to attend me in the surveying and, this being the only thing I was in need of, every matter has been soon arranged. I am only at present to regret that a heavy rain and thick mist which has been incessant ever since my arrival here, does put an insuperable obstacle to my wish of proceeding immediately to the survey.*[32]

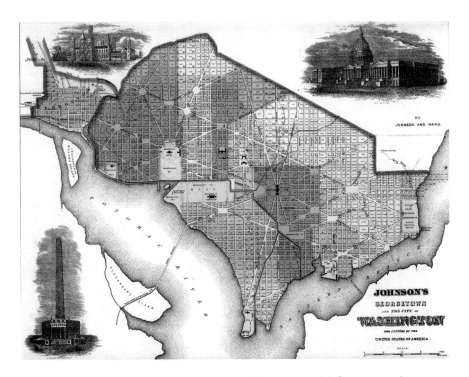

A map incorporating L'Enfant's original plan for Washington, with Georgetown drawn as a separate entity in the upper left. *Johnson and Ward, 1862. Courtesy Library of Congress, Geography and Map Division.*

Once L'Enfant and his associates got to work and accomplished the survey, President Washington came to Georgetown and held a dinner meeting with the landowners on whose property the capital would be located. The president negotiated compensation and other terms for transferring the acreage to the government. Several of the landowners lived in Georgetown, including Mayor Robert Peter, Thomas Beall of George, James Maccubin Lingan, Uriah Forrest, Benjamin Stoddert and Charles Beatty. Other property owners were added to the agreement later, including Samuel Davidson, William Deakins Jr., Thomas Johnson, Robert Lingan and John P. Van Ness.[33]

The commission overseeing the development of the Federal City worked with Washington, Jefferson and leaders of Congress in the spring of 1791 to appropriate funds for building a "Federal Hall," or Capitol building, a president's house and other government facilities. The planners also determined that streets going north–south in the new city would be numbered, with east–west streets designated by letters of the alphabet.

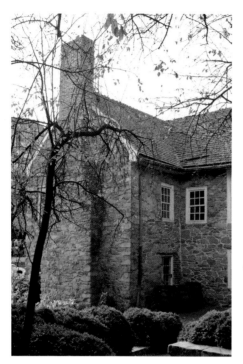

The Old Stone House, at 3051 M Street, built in 1765. Perhaps the oldest building in Georgetown, it is now operated as a museum by the National Park Service. It was rumored to have been used by L'Enfant as an office when he designed the city of Washington. *Photo by Missy Loewe.*

L'Enfant incorporated the street-naming directions into his map, along with grand avenues traversing the city diagonally and intersecting at large plazas. Most of the diagonal avenues were named for the states. The French-trained civil engineer aimed to give the Federal City distinctive design elements from the great cities of Europe to make America's capital as grand and beautiful as any other. To aid the effort, Jefferson supplied L'Enfant with maps of major European cities he had acquired while serving as America's minister to France.

L'Enfant lived at Suter's Tavern during his time in Georgetown. But historians are uncertain where he worked drawing his map and conducting other business, where Andrew Ellicott had his office as surveyor or where the three commissioners held their meetings. Popular speculation places L'Enfant's Georgetown headquarters at a small granite building called the Old Stone House, still standing at 3049 M Street, which some have called "General Washington's Headquarters." But because Washington never would have needed a military headquarters in Georgetown, and because he generally held his meetings at Suter's Tavern, a more probable theory is that the Old Stone House might have been the office of the commissioners.[34]

Wherever the office was, L'Enfant was said to have been an overbearing presence there. He constantly engaged in heated debates and disagreements with his colleagues and supervisors over almost every facet of the project. His grandiose visions, along with his temperamental nature and stubborn insistence on his version of perfection, proved to be his undoing amid the constrained resources and political sensitivities that often characterize government work.

He was late submitting the plan to President Washington, and he refused to take orders from anyone except the president, despite repeated pleas to accept guidance from the three commissioners of the District of Columbia: Thomas Johnson, David Stuart and Daniel Carroll. L'Enfant encountered particular friction with Stuart, who had recently married Mrs. John Parke Custis, the widowed daughter-in-law of First Lady Martha Washington. Things went from bad to worse when a nephew of Commissioner Carroll started building a house in the new city and L'Enfant had it demolished because it would have protruded into a street as laid out in his plan.

Later in the year, L'Enfant sent a long, detailed missive to President Washington, previewing the magnitude of the tasks ahead, estimating the cost at an eye-popping $1.2 million and outlining his terms "for renewing the work at the Federal City" in the approaching season. L'Enfant also was adamant that construction of the entire city be substantially complete before anyone would be allowed to move there or begin working in the new buildings.

"Unfortunately," his biographer noted, "L'Enfant did not realize the poverty of the Treasury; and the state of mind of national legislators, particularly of the North, who preferred to stay in Philadelphia, to moving 'to the Indian Place' on the banks of the Potomac." Shortly after filing his report to President Washington, L'Enfant either resigned under pressure or was fired.

"It is generally thought that the trouble concerning Daniel Carroll...was the reason for L'Enfant's resignation from the Washington work in March 1792, and the reason for the letter from Secretary of State Jefferson terminating his services that month," Ms. Ecker wrote. "But a close analysis of L'Enfant's experiences reveals that this was simply a 'serious incident' in a chain of troubles."[35]

L'Enfant dejectedly packed up and left Georgetown to pursue other projects, including a plan for the city of Patterson, New Jersey, and assignments to design a hotel in Philadelphia and a magnificent house for industrialist Robert Morris in the same city. He spent the next several years in legal disputes with the government over how much he should have been paid for his contributions to the capital. After his departure, L'Enfant's map of the Federal City was modified by Ellicott, who continued working from Georgetown with the commissioners to lay out the new capital and get construction underway.

AMERICA'S FIRST SUBURB

Life as a Bedroom Community

As the new capital city took shape across the creek, Georgetown's population swelled with a steady influx of laborers, engineers and craftsmen who trooped over the bridge each morning to their jobs at the construction sites, performing tasks such as surveying, bricklaying, roofing and carpentry. The daily back and forth must have been the first example of an American "bedroom community," where people live in one town and travel to work in another, arguably making Georgetown the nation's first suburb.

Work on the city of Washington, which the first president modestly referred to only by its earlier title of "Federal City," progressed steadily. A momentous milestone was achieved on September 18, 1792, with the laying of the cornerstone of the U.S. Capitol. Lengthy newspaper accounts describe the elaborate festivities marking the installation of the large sandstone block, which was personally cemented into place by George Washington in his capacity as president and as a Mason. A "brilliant crowd of spectators of both sexes" assembled for the observance, including "the Mayor and Corporation of George Town."

John Threlkeld was Georgetown's mayor at the time, and much of the "brilliant crowd" probably came from Georgetown as well, because "dwellers in the City of Washington at that time were few and far between." Another landmark event came less than a month later, at noon on October 12, 1792, when the cornerstone of the president's house was laid. No written records of any major celebration survive. Perhaps it was too soon after the elaborate Capitol ceremony to make time for another big gathering.[36]

Despite the disagreements that prompted L'Enfant's departure, George Washington, at least to some degree, shared the French architect's vision of a world-class capital. The president predicted that "a century hence, if this country keeps united, it will produce a city, though not so large as London, yet of a magnitude inferior to few others in Europe."[37]

Work progressed on the new city for several years, with most of the laborers and supervisors continuing to commute from Georgetown. Among the government officials living in Georgetown during the construction period was Thomas Jefferson, who moved there in 1792 while serving as the first secretary of state and official overseer of L'Enfant and his successors. George Washington also paid several visits to Georgetown and the job sites across the creek to check on the progress, even after his term as president ended in 1797.

George Washington never got to preside in the new Capitol or reside in the executive mansion. The first commander in chief to live and work in the city of Washington was John Adams. As the Federal City neared completion, former President Washington's friends and admirers in Georgetown honored him with a banquet that turned into one of the town's most heavily attended social events in years. A newspaper ad announcing the gala, dubbed a "Birthnight Ball," read:

> *The Ladies and Gentlemen of George Town and its vicinity are informed that there will be a Ball at the Union Tavern on Friday the 22nd instant (Feb. 22, 1799), in honor of Lieutenant-General George Washington. At request of the Managers.—John Suter, Jr.*

The crowd was so large that the tavern could not hold all the well-wishers, and the merriment spilled into the streets and lasted into the wee hours. The Birthnight Balls, instituted around the end of the Revolutionary War to celebrate Washington's birthday, evolved into one of the new country's first national holidays, along with the Fourth of July.[38]

Georgetown clearly felt a kinship with George Washington, and folks were fond of sharing their many stories about personal contacts with the father of their country. One of the more popular was the tale of schoolboy Francis Dodge, who had moved from Massachusetts to Georgetown with his family. One day in 1798, the youngster was tying up his small rowboat at the main public wharf when he noticed an elderly man scurrying down the street and onto the dock. The old fellow, appearing to be in quite a hurry, asked the boy whether the ferry was about to arrive. The lad replied that it had just left and then, recognizing the exceedingly disappointed gentleman as George Washington, offered to row him across the river in his own little boat.

The former president gratefully accepted. During the trip, Washington asked the boy his name. "Francis Dodge, sir," Dodge replied, prompting the general to inquire, "By any chance related to Colonel Robert Dodge, who served so gallantly with me during the war?"

"Yes, General, he was my father," Francis proudly answered while working the oars.

"Oh, indeed!" Washington exclaimed. "I am greatly pleased to know you, young man. You must come to Mount Vernon sometime to see me."

No one knows whether Francis Dodge ever visited Mount Vernon before Washington's death the next year, but the youngster grew up to become one of Georgetown's leading citizens, and years later, his grandson, Colonel Harrison H. Dodge, worked for forty years as the superintendent of the Washington family's Mount Vernon estate.[39]

By 1800, construction of the Federal City had made sufficient progress, and the government was ready to move in. The arduous task began of transferring the people, equipment and records of the United States government from Philadelphia to its new home. The massive migration was another boost to Georgetown's status as the capital's bedroom community. The lack of residential accommodations around the federal office buildings in Washington forced the new arrivals to seek homes for themselves and their families outside the city, but still as close as possible to their new workplace.

The nearest major city, Baltimore, was about forty miles away, a daunting commute in the days of horse-powered travel. That left Alexandria and Georgetown as the only practical alternatives. Alexandria required either a long excursion by boat or an overland trip covering a six-mile stretch of road on horseback or by carriage, followed by a ferry ride across the river. So Georgetown, just across Rock Creek and only about three miles from the Capitol building, instantly became the neighborhood of choice, with its ready supply of substantial housing and its well-established commercial district and social scene.

Georgetown's importance as Washington's closest bedroom community is illustrated in a letter that Treasury Secretary Oliver Wolcott wrote his wife in July 1800 after arriving in Washington. Wolcott related his impressions of the new capital, both good and bad, and contrasted "this famous place, the permanent seat of American government," to his family's former home in Connecticut.

"The situation is pleasant, and indeed beautiful," he wrote.

The prospects are equal to those which are called good on Connecticut River. The soil here is called good, but I call it bad. It is an exceedingly stiff reddish clay, which becomes dust in dry and mortar in rainy weather. The President's House was built to be looked at by visitors and strangers, and will render its occupant an object of ridicule with some, and of pity with others. It must be cold and damp in winter, and cannot be kept in tolerable order without a regiment of servants.

There is one good tavern about forty rods from the Capitol, and several other houses are built and erecting, but I do not perceive how the members of Congress can possibly secure lodgings, unless they will consent to live like scholars in a college or monks in a monastery, crowded ten or twenty in one house, and utterly excluded from society. The only resource for such as wish to live comfortably will, I think, be found in Georgetown, three miles distant, over as bad a road in winter as the clay grounds near Hartford.

Within the city of Washington, Wolcott told his wife,

there are, in fact, but few houses, at any one place, and most of them small miserable huts, which present an awful contrast to the public buildings. The people are poor, and as far as I can judge, they live like fishes, by eating each other. All of the ground for several miles around the city being, in the opinion of the people, too valuable to be cultivated, remains unfenced. There are but few enclosures even for gardens, and those are in bad order. You may look in almost any direction, over an extent of ground nearly as large as the city of New York, without seeing a fence or any object except brick-kilns and temporary huts for laborers.

In addition to the housing shortage and bad roads, the city of Washington was difficult to locate, particularly when traveling over land. Even President Adams's family, moving to their new home in November 1800, had trouble finding the place and getting all of their belongings safely delivered to the executive mansion.

In a letter to her daughter, First Lady Abigail Adams wrote that she arrived in Washington

without meeting with any accident worth noticing, except losing ourselves when we left Baltimore and going eight or nine miles out the Frederick road, by which means we were obliged to go the other eight through woods, where we wandered two hours without finding a guide or the path.

Woods are all you see from Baltimore until you reach the city—which is only in name. Here and there is a small hut, without a glass window, interspersed amongst the forests, through which you travel miles without seeing any human being. In the city there are buildings enough, if they were compact and finished, to accommodate Congress and those attached to it, but as they are, I see no great comfort for them.[40]

Mrs. Adams penned another letter the same month describing the difficulties of the first family's move into the opulent new presidential residence:

The vessel which has my clothes and other matters is not arrived. I have no looking-glasses but dwarfs for this house, nor a twentieth part lamps enough to light it. Many things were stolen, many were broken, by the removal; among the number my tea china is more than half missing. My rooms are very pleasant and warm whilst the doors of the hall are closed. You can scarce believe that here in this wilderness city I should find my time so occupied as it is. My visitors come, some of them, three and four miles. To return one of them is the work of a day.[41]

Many of Mrs. Adams's visitors came from Georgetown, where most of her husband's colleagues in Congress and the administration were making their homes.

All the while it served as host city for the planning and building of Washington, Georgetown's export business for tobacco and other farm products had been moving ahead as well. Housing construction intensified in every part of town to meet the needs of new residents. Taverns, shops and eateries became more crowded. The streets were jammed with a diverse mix of people: merchants, businessmen, sailors, dockworkers, farmers, government officials, construction workers, travelers, diplomats, schoolchildren and a growing number of African slaves.

New stores, churches, banks, schools and other establishments appeared along the waterfront, and new neighborhoods began spreading outward from the original town. With the swelling population came the inevitable urban problems of overcrowding, sanitation, safety and crime. Civic leaders struggled to address the nettlesome challenges.

As early as 1784, the expanding number of school-age children prompted creative schemes to find and fund new classroom space. An advertisement in the *Maryland Gazette* promoted a *lottery for raising $1,400 to be applied to the purchasing of a house for the use of the George Town Academy. The right education of youth is an object of such vast importance of freedom and happiness that there needs no strength of reasoning to recommend the above scheme, which is meant to promote it to the patronage and encouragement of a liberal public.*

The challenges of transportation for commuters also were pursued by various entrepreneurs, including a businessman named James Bull, who launched an early mass-transit project connecting the three cities in the federal district by boat during the busy capital construction period. Bull placed an ad in the June 26, 1795 *Impartial Observer and Washington Advertiser* telling passengers that his water-going bus would

leave George Town every morning at seven o'clock and call at this place (City of Washington) on her way to Alexandria. Leave Alexandria every evening at 4 and call on way to George Town. 17 cents from George Town to Greenleaf Point, 33 to Alexandria. Passages engaged at Mr. Suter's or Mr. Semmes' Tavern in George Town. [42]

Horse-drawn stagecoaches also became popular modes of travel, with taverns usually serving as the stations. An advertisement in the *Sentinel of Liberty* newspaper on June 27, 1800, announced that "stages will leave Light-Lane Number 3 adjoining the Fountain Inn every day (Monday excepted). Returning, leave Mr. Heiskell's, Alexandria, at 3 o'clock. Mr. Semmes' at George Town at 5." [43]

To keep commuters safe, the town passed a law that ferryboats "must not have pendent or any other colour flying or ring a bell on board so as to affrighten the horses and thereby endanger the lives of the passengers. Penalty of $20." To protect pedestrians, a law directed

that any person who shall by galloping, or otherwise force at an improper speed any Horse, Mare, or Gelding, shall if a free man, forfeit and pay for every such offence the sum of 15 shillings current money; if an apprentice, servant or a slave the master or the mistress shall forfeit and pay the sum of 7 shillings and sixpence.

Another public safety ordinance prohibited "the going at large of geese and swine" in Georgetown and made it

*lawful to kill any such and give notice to the Mayor or one of the Aldermen,
the offender to be sent to the public market house where the owner may claim
within four hours, or if no claim in four hours, the finder take and apply
to proper use. All goats running at large shall be forfeited to who ever shall
take them up.*

To safeguard public sanitation, there was a thirty-shilling fine on allowing
too much garbage, particularly glass bottles or oyster shells, to pile up "in
quantity" on any property in town.[44]

To curb the frowned-upon practice of unlicensed gambling, an October
1803 ordinance warned that

*any person or persons who shall keep or maintain the common gaming house
or open or set up any public gaming table shall forfeit and pay $20 current
money. Provided always, that licensed billiard tables are not intended hereby
to be prohibited or herein included.*

In 1807, the city adopted a fairly complex ordinance to

*more effectually diminish the number of dogs in Georgetown as they have
become a public nuisance; on the first dog of the male kind owned by any
one person, $1; on the second, $2; and on all over two, owned by the same
person, $5; and on the first of the female kind, $2; on the second, $4;
and on all dogs of the female kind over and above two, owned by the same
person, $10.*[45]

Several laws and regulations placed stiffer restrictions on the city's African
slaves than on white residents. One law directed that "no slave shall be
permitted to sell any article whatever (other than fruit) on the Sabbath." A
1796 ordinance aimed at curtailing cock fighting read:

*Whereas, many respectable inhabitants of Georgetown have complained
that they suffer great inconvenience from the vast concourse of idle white and
black persons that frequently assemble together for the purpose of fighting
cocks, at which time they drink to excess, become riotous, and disturb the
quiet and repose of the good citizens, be it ordained by Mayor, Recorder,
Aldermen, and Common Council that any white person or persons or free
negro or negroes who shall presume to fight any game cocks or dunghill fowls
within the jurisdiction of the corporation for any wagers or for diversion*

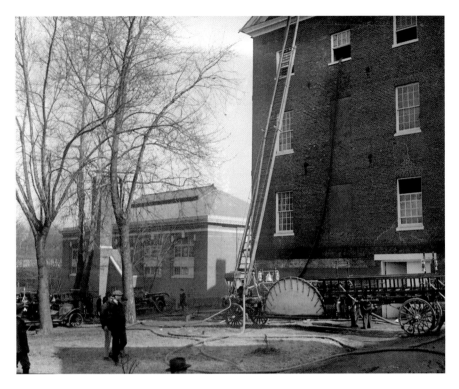

Fires were a problem throughout the history of Georgetown. The community organized numerous fire brigades and companies to battle blazes at homes and businesses. This fire erupted on the Georgetown University campus in 1921. *National Photo Company Collection, 1921 (reproduction number 03481). Courtesy Library of Congress, Prints and Photographs Division.*

shall for every offense pay $5. Also if having assembled in a disorderly manner for the purpose of fighting cocks, if they refuse to disperse, constables shall take such negro or negroes (being slaves) and give him, her, or them, due correction upon the bare back in some public part of Georgetown not exceeding 39 strikes.[46]

The city's rapid growth also made it necessary to boost the staffing of the police and fire departments. With Georgetown's close-together houses and dense population, fires were a major problem. The first official Georgetown fire company was formed in 1803, when a horse-drawn fire engine was purchased and a law was passed requiring all homeowners to keep special leather fire buckets on every floor of their dwellings, "to be numbered and the name of the owner painted on them, to be used in time of fire, and to contain not less than two and one-half gallons of water."[47]

While most blazes began in kitchens or factories, or were ignited by unattended candles or lanterns, one of Georgetown's most spectacular infernos began onboard a ship in the harbor.

On May 21, 1791, a freighter called the *Termagent* was anchored in the Potomac when smoke was seen drifting from one of its lower decks. A large crowd of residents and sailors raced to the wharf to organize a fire brigade but quickly retreated when someone remembered that the ship was loaded with gunpowder. As flames consumed the vessel, a terrific explosion suddenly shot a billowing mushroom cloud of burning debris into the sky and shook the entire town like an earthquake. Terrified residents bolted from their trembling houses as thick black smoke churned across the city and crackling embers rained down on the rooftops. Cinders flew in every direction, igniting fires in buildings along the waterfront, including a large tobacco warehouse. The contingent of firefighters who had wisely opted against boarding the flaming ship began patrolling the town to douse the blazes onshore.[48]

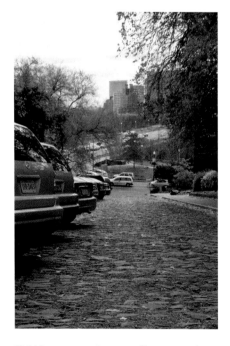

Cobblestones used to pave Georgetown's muddy streets in colonial times still survive throughout the community. The paving stones often were taken from piles of ballast material left along the Potomac shoreline by cargo ships. *Photo by Missy Loewe.*

In addition to beefing up the firefighting capabilities, civic leaders also embarked on other notable public works projects, including an effort to pave Georgetown's muddy streets. The town formed a committee in 1801 to devise a plan for installing paving stones on main thoroughfares and gradually extending pavement to the city's side streets. In 1810, the town installed oil-fueled streetlamps on select corners to enable residents "to find their way to and from church on a dark night."[49] In 1811, city officials laid the cornerstone for Georgetown's first public school to provide education to children whose families could not afford the town's private academies.[50]

While Georgetown's taverns had served as centers for public business and social activity for many years, the expanding population gave rise

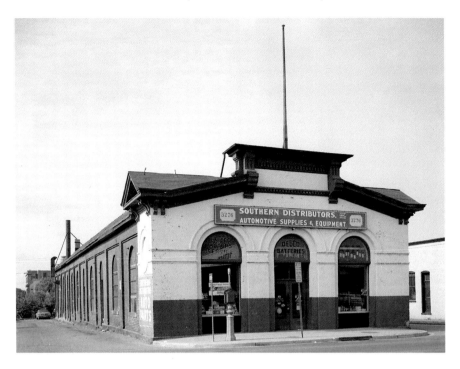

The old Market House, once a focal point of shopping and social activity in the community, survives as an upscale shopping and dining complex at 3276 M Street. The structure's original foundation was built in 1796 for use as a warehouse. *Courtesy Library of Congress.*

to a new focal point of community life: the public market. A group of local farmers and merchants established the city's first major "market house" about 1806 near the waterfront. The sprawling building, with stalls selling meat, fruit, vegetables and all sorts of other goods and household items, quickly became the busiest place in the city to shop and socialize.[51]

Georgetown closed out the eighteenth century with the death of its most famous frequent visitor, George Washington. The general died of a fever at Mount Vernon on the cold night of December 14, 1799, at age sixty-seven, in the last month of the last century that he had been so instrumental in shaping. The city plunged into mourning, and the Reverend Stephen Bloomer Balch, founder of the Georgetown Presbyterian Church where Washington had often worshiped, announced a special open-air service to commemorate the life of the former president. More than one thousand sorrow-stricken residents—about one-third of Georgetown's population—turned out to hear Balch's elegant eulogy for his friend and America's founding father.

OFF TO BATTLE, UP IN FLAMES

The War of 1812

While no Revolutionary War battles were fought near Georgetown, its proximity to the new American capital put it much closer to military action during the War of 1812. A number of Georgetown residents who served heroically in the Revolution signed up for service again when Congress declared war against Britain on June 18 of that year. The British already were fighting in Europe against the French empire of Napoleon, so England wanted to impede U.S. trade with France. Officials in Washington also accused the British of forming military alliances with several Indian tribes to hinder America's westward expansion.

A major contributor to the U.S. war effort was Georgetown foundry owner Henry Foxhall, who came to the capital area in 1799 and built an ordnance factory just behind the campus of Georgetown College. Foxhall became close friends with Thomas Jefferson, with whom he shared a love of tinkering with mechanical devices and playing the violin.

Foxhall's foundry, the only one south of Philadelphia, became an important supplier of artillery for the American forces. Foxhall was said to be the only founder in America "who understood the proper mode of cannon manufacture" and began the first U.S. production of the newly developed bored cannon, the most technologically advanced weapon of the day. Many older cannons were melted down and recast using Foxhall's method.

Foxhall's cannons were considered so superior that Commodore Oliver Hazard Perry of the U.S. Navy refused to go into combat without them. The pivotal battle of Lake Erie was deferred until Foxhall could *fill an order from the government for guns, and transport them over the mountains on carts drawn by 10 or 12 yoke of oxen to the scene of the engagement. From the deck of his flagship, the* Lawrence, *manned by the guns from Georgetown, Perry sent his famous message, "We have met the enemy and they are ours!"*[52]

Foxhall later became Georgetown's mayor.

A local hero since the days of the Revolution was General James Maccubbin Lingan, another Scotsman who struck it rich in the tobacco business. As a young lieutenant in the Continental army, Lingan was severely injured when an enemy soldier jabbed a bayonet into his chest. He was captured and held on a British prison ship, where many of his fellow inmates died. When a coffin was brought for one of them, it was found to be too short, and the guards started to decapitate the body to make it fit. Outraged, the wounded Lingan stood defiantly over the corpse, vowing to kill any redcoat who dared behead the dead soldier. The guards gave in and brought a larger casket.

During Lingan's custody, Sir Samuel Hood, a British admiral who also was Lingan's cousin, came aboard the prison ship and offered the American lieutenant the handsome sum of two thousand British pounds and a high rank in His Majesty's army for switching sides. "I'll rot here first!" the enraged Lingan roared back. This reaction got the disdainful prisoner confined to such a small compartment that he was unable to stand fully upright for months after his release. But he continued serving throughout the Revolution, eventually attaining the rank of general.

In the election year of 1812, Lingan was a supporter of the Federalist political party, whose official newspaper, the *Federal Republican*, was under attack for publishing editorials sympathetic to the British side. Not long after the War of 1812 was declared, mobs of angry protesters stormed the newspaper's Baltimore office, smashing furniture and equipment, pelting staff members with rocks and other projectiles and taunting them with vicious shouts of "Tory! Tory!"

Lingan, who had traveled from Georgetown to help save the paper, came forward to address the frenzied crowd, angrily tore open his shirt to reveal the purple scar from his British bayonet wound and bellowed, "Does this look as if I was a traitor?" Just then, an enraged protester hurled a stone that struck Lingan squarely in the deep chest scar. He fell to the floor and died a short time later—an early martyr, some said, to the basic American principle of freedom of the press.[53]

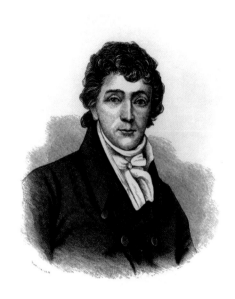

Georgetown district attorney Francis Scott
Key (1779–1843), who wrote "The Star-
Spangled Banner" during the War of 1812.
Courtesy Library of Congress.

News of General Lingan's ugly death sent Georgetown into grief, and because no church in town could accommodate the crowd, his funeral was held outdoors in Montrose Park, atop the city's highest hill, on September 1, 1812. At the front of the gathering, the tent used by George Washington during the Revolution was erected to shelter the clergymen, family and other dignitaries. The eulogy was delivered by Lingan's friend George Washington Parke Custis, a grandson of Martha Washington. Lingan's riderless horse was led solemnly behind the casket in the funeral cortege, followed by two of the general's fellow Revolutionary War heroes from Georgetown, Major Benjamin Stoddert and Colonel Philip Stuart.[54]

Georgetown's most famous figure in the War of 1812 was district attorney and part-time poet Francis Scott Key. One of eleven children from a well-known family of lawyers, Key occasionally wrote verses to entertain relatives and friends. During the British blockade of Baltimore Harbor on September 13, 1814, Key learned that his friend Dr. William Beanes had been captured. Key traveled to Baltimore and went aboard a British man-of-war to negotiate the doctor's release, unaware that the bombardment of Fort McHenry was about to begin. The ship's captain, fearing that Key might alert the Americans to the pending attack, detained him onboard. Key stood anxiously on deck all night long as British bombs and rockets relentlessly pounded the American fort.

When dawn came and the smoke cleared, Key noticed that the fort's oversized American flag, although ripped and tattered by bullets, was still fluttering proudly in the morning breeze. The sight inspired him to compose a poem called "The Star-Spangled Banner," which later was put to music by his friends at the Georgetown Glee Club and became America's national anthem.[55]

Georgetown's closest brush with combat during the War of 1812 came on the night of August 14, 1814, when British troops marched into Washington and set fire to the Capitol, the Library of Congress, the Treasury Department, the president's house and other public buildings. When word of the "Burning of Washington" reached Georgetown, residents feared that the attack might spread into their neighborhoods as well. Men of the city braced for battle, while wives, children and hundreds of other spectators climbed the steep ridge called the Heights of Georgetown, which offered a panoramic view of the president's house and Capitol just down the river. The onlookers gasped in fear and disbelief as America's capital city went up in flames, casting a haunting orange glow across the overcast night sky.

Among the grand homes that lined the Heights of Georgetown was a mansion called Tudor Place, owned by businessman and tobacco heir Thomas Peter, son of the city's first mayor, and his wife, Martha Parke Custis, a granddaughter of Martha Washington. The stately yellow-colored stone residence had been designed by William Thornton, a family friend who also was the architect of the U.S. Capitol building. While their husbands headed out to defend the town, Mrs. Peter and Mrs. Thornton spent the harrowing evening sitting side by side at a large front window of Tudor Place, looking down tearfully as the city, which Mrs. Peter's adopted grandfather had envisioned and Mrs. Thornton's husband had helped design, went up in flames. The odious infernos raged into the night, until a severe thunderstorm—some called it a hurricane or a tornado—lashed the area with lightning and sheets of driving rain that drowned the fires and sent the British fleeing.[56]

While Mrs. Peter and Mrs. Thornton watched from Tudor Place, another prestigious home on the Heights of Georgetown was taking in a very important refugee from the British invasion. First Lady Dolley Madison had been preparing to host a dinner party at the executive mansion when she heard that the attack was underway. She immediately canceled the event and began feverishly packing as many valuables and documents as she could before fleeing the president's house, which she managed to do just moments ahead of the redcoats' arrival.

Mrs. Madison was particularly worried about a famous full-length portrait of George Washington by artist Gilbert Stuart. When she discovered that the large picture was bolted firmly to the wall, she ordered staff members to break the frame and pull out the canvas. After handing the painting over to friends for safekeeping, the first lady jumped into a wagon driven

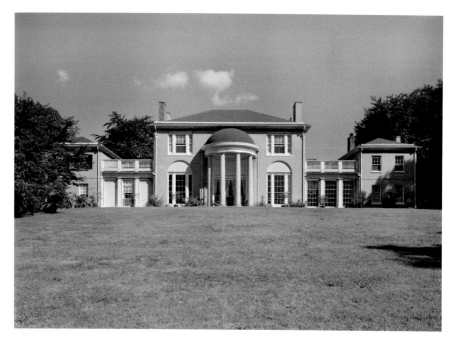

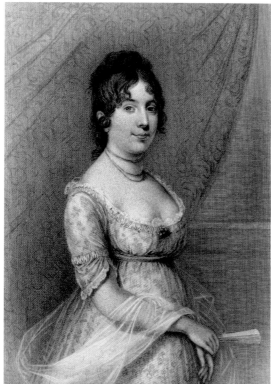

Above: The Tudor Place mansion, 1644 Thirty-first Street, was built by early tobacco merchants. The house, designed by the same architect as the U.S. Capitol, was the home of several generations of descendants of Martha Washington. *HABS (reproduction number HABS DC, GEO, 2-5). Courtesy Library of Congress, Prints and Photographs Division.*

Left: First Lady Dolley Madison (1768–1849), who took refuge in Georgetown after fleeing the White House when the British burned Washington during the War of 1812. This portrait is by artist Gilbert Stuart, who also painted the famous likeness of George Washington that Mrs. Madison rescued from the White House as British troops approached. *Courtesy Library of Congress.*

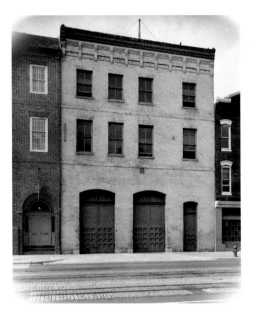

The original headquarters of the Columbia Bank, 3208–10 M Street, built in 1796, where Secretary of State James Monroe came for a loan to finance the financially strapped U.S. government to fund General Andrew Jackson's Battle of New Orleans campaign in the War of 1812. *Marc Blair, 1966. Courtesy Library of Congress.*

by family friend Charles Carroll, who then sped toward his home in Georgetown. Carroll was a cousin of a former U.S. senator, also named Charles Carroll, who had served with Madison in the Continental Congress and signed the Declaration of Independence as a delegate from Maryland. Mrs. Madison stayed at the Carroll home, a handsome brick mansion called Bellevue, until she could be reunited with the president. When the executive residence was rebuilt, its fire-charred stone walls were painted white, prompting the building to become known as the White House.[57]

After the Burning of Washington, the U.S. Treasury was running short of cash. Late in 1814, in a desperate effort to secure funds for the war effort, Secretary of State James Monroe rode into Georgetown on horseback to visit the Columbia Bank. Monroe explained to banker William Whann that the government was broke and needed help paying for General Andrew Jackson's upcoming mission to New Orleans, where the British were blockading the harbor. When Monroe pledged his own private fortune as collateral, Whann granted the loan.

With funding secured, Jackson marched south and won a major victory at the Battle of New Orleans on January 8, 1815, unaware that a peace treaty ending hostilities had been signed two weeks earlier on Christmas Eve. Nevertheless, Jackson's triumph was widely celebrated and made him a national hero, eventually propelling him to the presidency.[58]

PLAGUES OF PROGRESS

Floods, Fires, Freezes and Bugs

B usiness boomed in Georgetown in the decades following the War of 1812. The rebuilding of Washington after its torching by the British meant more work for the businesses and laborers of the capital's closest suburb. The tobacco trade and other shipping concerns also continued to prosper, bringing new residents and more money into the city. Moreover, the task of running America's new government was developing into a substantial industry as well, and Georgetown's proximity, elegant housing and lively social scene made it a magnet for incoming bureaucrats, politicians and diplomats.

The tobacco business was doing so well that in 1822, the city approved the construction of two new warehouses, to be designed as "fire-proof," with thick brick walls, slate roofs and sheet-iron shutters and doors. The cavernous buildings, which held several thousand hogsheads of tobacco, were still unable to keep pace with the surging demand. So the city built even more facilities. Tobacco exporting remained strong for most years until the 1830s, when prices declined and much of the business community turned to more profitable pursuits, such as milling flour and processing cotton, which was gaining popularity as a cash crop. A heavy trade in coal also developed to fuel manufacturing plants and large oceangoing ships that were converting to steam power.

Two large merchant ships, the *Eagle* and the *Shenandoah*, were based at the port and sailed regularly between Georgetown and Europe, leaving with large loads of tobacco and returning with cargos of salt and other merchandise

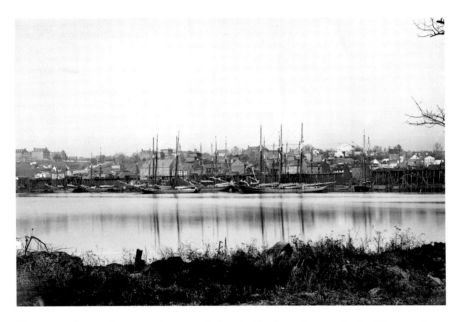

Georgetown's waterfront was often crowded with ships from Europe, the Caribbean and other American ports, bringing merchandise from abroad and leaving with cargos of tobacco and other products. *William Morris Smith, 1865. Courtesy Library of Congress.*

from abroad. When both vessels were lost at sea, a number of enterprising citizens purchased four other ships named the *Francis Depuu*, the *Southerner*, the *Caledonia* and the *Catherine Jackson*, all of which went into service in 1836 to handle the escalating transatlantic commerce.

Georgetown merchants also continued to build the "coasting trade" with Boston, New York and other cities on the eastern seaboard, and lively commerce with the Caribbean brought in products such as sugar and rum. The shipping business was so brisk that the Georgetown waterfront frequently resembled a forest of masts. Port records show that during the year 1835, about three thousand ships pulled into Georgetown harbor, transporting nearly 200,000 tons of freight.[59]

All of the new and expanding business was making Georgetown a major financial center, and new banks began appearing in the city, including the Farmers and Mechanics Bank, founded in 1814 by William Marbury, who became its first president. Marbury had gained notoriety several years earlier in a dispute that led to one of the most important early decisions by the U.S. Supreme Court. President John Adams had appointed Marbury as justice of the peace for the federal territory, but the paperwork ratifying

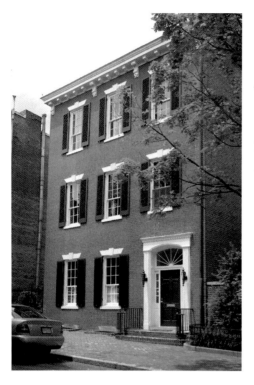

This former home of banker William Marbury at 3307 N Street was purchased in the 1950s by Massachusetts senator John F. Kennedy, who lived in the house until he became president. *Photo by Missy Loewe.*

the job assignment had not been formally delivered before the next president, Thomas Jefferson, took office.

Presenting such documents to new officeholders was the job of the secretary of state, who, after Jefferson took office, was James Madison. But because Jefferson opposed the appointment, Madison never made the delivery. Marbury sued, and the case went to the Supreme Court, which declared the law under which Adams made the appointment to be unconstitutional. This was the first time America's highest court ever struck down a law. Chief Justice John Marshall's words from the landmark ruling, which established the concept of judicial review, are etched into the marble wall of the U.S. Supreme Court building: "It is emphatically the province and duty of the Judicial Department to say what the law is.—Marbury vs. Madison, 1803." Marbury never got his justice of the peace job, but he did enjoy a long and distinguished financial career.

As banks and other new businesses—including shops, factories, offices, warehouses and shipping facilities—appeared, along with new houses for all of the people who worked in them, Georgetown found itself facing more issues of traffic, sanitation, utility services, crime and fire protection. One of the most troubling concerns amid the river port's galloping prosperity was the problem of poverty. The mayor and council appointed a commission in May 1826 to serve as "board of trustees for the poor of Georgetown." With funding assistance from Congress, the city established shelters and other accommodations for the less fortunate, and in 1831, construction began on the Georgetown Poor House.

The large two-story complex, dedicated with much religious fanfare, had "an imposing appearance as seen from the road," with staff quarters, kitchens and separate dormitories and dining rooms for boys and girls. The main building was surrounded by orchards and gardens tended by the residents, which supplied the poorhouse kitchens and also produced fruit and vegetables to sell at the local market to help defray costs. Proud city officials professed that "the house and grounds showed a flourishing condition that was captivating to the visitor."

While life at the poorhouse provided safe shelter and good meals, some new residents were subjected to a harrowing initiation, as described by nineteenth-century Georgetown commentator Richard Plummer Jackson, who often referred to himself in his writings as "the chronicler":

> *They had a custom of washing oft' every person who was committed to the poor-house by the police magistrate of the town, by stripping them of their clothing, whether the weather was cold or warm, and standing them in a tall chimney, two stories high, when a man would carry up a large bucket of water and pour the contents upon the head and body of the prisoner. The consequence, if the weather was cold, was a chilly reception, and in two cases, to the chronicler's knowledge, when the shower hath had been used upon individuals who were committed for intemperance, in cold weather,* were attacked with mania a potu [delirium or insanity often linked to alcoholism in those days] *and died from its effects.*

In tandem with the poorhouse, the city also operated a Home Industrial School to instruct needy young men in "the habits of industry, that will carry them forward into any pursuit in life," Jackson wrote, adding that Georgetown's early exercise in social services "carried gladness to the hearts of many families who, otherwise, would have suffered for want of the necessaries of life."[60]

Another problem plaguing Georgetown since its earliest days was fire protection. Since the first fire department was formed back in 1803, Georgetown's municipal fire companies had managed to successfully douse many of the blazes that had erupted around town. But with urban expansion, fire was becoming a larger issue, and for the tobacco warehouses and other large businesses, it was a major threat. To meet the heightening challenges, the city purchased a new fire engine in 1817. Nicknamed the Vigilant, the bulky, horse-drawn vehicle was equipped to dispatch firemen, their tools and a large supply of water.

To illustrate the seriousness of Georgetown's fire problem, "chronicler" Jackson listed about one hundred major blazes that he personally recalled from the 1800s, including

> *a row of brick houses on the south side of First Street, belonging to the late Bank of the United States...the bakehouse and warehouse of White & Mumby, with their stock of groceries,* [a multi-block fire] *that was checked in its course by the fireproof warehouse of John Kurtz, now occupied by John M. May, but from that north to First Street all the buildings were destroyed...the fine old Union Hotel on Bridge Street...John Lawrence's skin dressing establishment on Fayette Street; burnt three times...Hick's cabinet store and shop, which burnt three times...the "Cedars," residence of Colonel Cox...J.S. Tourse & Bomford's large flour mill...a soap and grease factory, situated on Water Street...the fine residence of the late Commodore Cassin on Beall Street..."Carter Place," occupied by the French Minister, Count de Sartiges, and formerly by John F. Crampton, envoy from England...William H. Hazel's livery stable...and Ramsburg & Sons' sumac mill and skin dressing establishment, situated near the Alexandria Aqueduct* [in addition to several tobacco warehouses].[61]

To keep pace with the frequent fires, Georgetown added four new firefighting organizations beginning in 1819, called the Columbian, Mechanical, Western Star and Eagle companies. Each entity owned fire engines equipped with large water tanks and pumps operated by long iron levers with wooden arms, "to be worked by the strength of the men in throwing water from the engines." It was strenuous labor, and a backup crew always stood ready to take over when the first pumping squad became exhausted.

To raise public awareness of fire safety and show off their fancy new vehicles, fire companies from Georgetown and Washington organized a great parade on October 24, 1837. It was an unseasonably hot day during a long dry spell, and "throngs of people who had come from miles around" lined the parade route under a broiling sun. There was "no hydrant water from the Potomac at that day, and the wells were pumped dry to supply the thirsty multitude who came from the surrounding country to witness the grand pageant." Fortunately, no major fires broke out during the procession.[62]

Another harrowing problem was frequent epidemics. Diseases such as yellow fever, cholera, smallpox and malaria, often brought by sailors from the many ships visiting the port, swept the population again and again through the years, causing widespread death, particularly among children. Vaccines and effective treatments were still mostly unknown, and medical science had not linked diseases to food-storage practices or mosquito bites, making outbreaks of contagious illness a major public fear.

Also on the list of local concerns, particularly in the business community, was keeping Georgetown's economy healthy and growing. In the late 1820s, a drop in tobacco exports and competition from other shipping ports prompted civic leaders to move ahead with one of the largest public works projects in American history up until that time: the Chesapeake and Ohio (C&O) Canal. The idea, envisioned several years earlier as a way to get more goods from upriver to Georgetown's port, was to create a new waterway linking the Potomac to the Ohio River. The canal would let boats bypass the Potomac's falls and rapids with a series of locks and dams that would connect the two river systems and build a stronger shipping business for both.

When Congress approved the canal plan, Georgetown residents giddily snatched up shares of stock being sold to finance the construction, believing that it would bring vast riches to them personally, as well as to the city. The stock sale sent Georgetown into "high glee," with bonfires and celebrations in the streets. The official groundbreaking for the canal came on Friday, the Fourth of July, 1828. President John Quincy Adams, accompanied by cabinet secretaries, diplomats, city officials and top brass of the canal company, marched to the ceremony site with the Marine Band blaring patriotic tunes and townspeople cheering along the way.

Adams proudly hoisted a shiny ceremonial shovel into the air and quoted a line of scripture, in which God instructs mankind to "be fruitful, and multiply, and replenish the earth, and subdue it." The president told the crowd that

> to subdue the earth was, therefore, one of the first duties assigned to man at his creation; and now, in his fallen condition, it remains among the most excellent of his occupations. To subdue the earth is pre-eminently the purposes of the undertaking, to the accomplishment of which the first stroke of the spade is now to be struck. That it is to be struck, by this hand, I invite you to witness.

The commander in chief then dramatically plunged the shovel toward the ground, but instead of slicing into the soil, it made a dull thud and bounced off a tree root just below the surface. When he made a second try and still hit the root, "a wag in the crowd cried out that he had come across a hickory

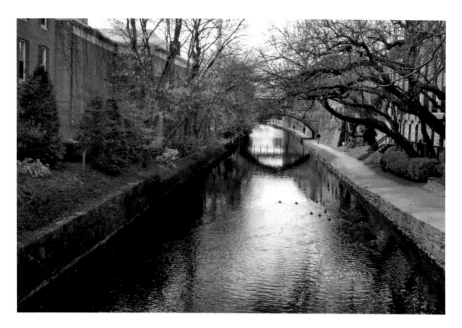

The Chesapeake and Ohio Canal boosted water transportation in the Georgetown region, allowing coal and agricultural products to bypass the falls just upstream. The canal was intended to connect the Potomac with the Ohio River system. The waterway never reached the Ohio system because competition from the railroads forced cancellation of the project's final phase. *Photo by Missy Loewe.*

root," a sarcastic reference to Adams's political rival, Andrew Jackson, known by the nickname "Old Hickory." The heckling prompted the president to slam down the spade, throw off his jacket, grab the shovel again and begin digging wildly at a slightly different spot, slinging streams of dirt into the air and drawing raucous hurrahs from the onlookers. The president closed the festivities by predicting glorious success for America's unprecedented engineering marvel, declaring that "the wonders of the ancient world, the pyramids of Egypt, the colossus of Rhodes, the temple of Ephesus, the mausoleum of Artemisia, the wall of China, sink into insignificance before it." The president's enthusiasm could have been inspired by personal economic interests. Adams had several local business affiliations, including ownership of a flour mill on Rock Creek, that stood to benefit from better water transport in the region.[63]

Building the canal took several years, and Georgetown was the scene of some serious construction accidents, including a collapse that killed two workers, some miscalculated dynamite explosions that sent rocks flying through nearby windows and a blast that heaved a fourteen-hundred-pound boulder onto a passing horse, killing it instantly. Violent public indignation over the horse incident prompted the explosives contractor to flee town.

Despite the setbacks, work progressed steadily, and on July 4, 1831, water was let into the first segment of the new channel. Phase one of the canal connecting Georgetown to Cumberland, Maryland, 184 miles away, was finished in 1850. The first shipment was a barge load of coal. The canal—with seventy-three locks, each one hundred feet long and fifteen feet wide, with eight feet of lift—carried countless tons of cargo through the years.

While it significantly boosted local commerce, the canal never fully lived up to its heady long-term expectations, and its shareholders never got the riches they envisioned. Competition from another new mode of transportation, the railroads, siphoned off so much of the canal's anticipated revenue that the C&O company canceled plans to continue digging onward toward the Ohio River.

The Georgetown-to-Cumberland stretch of the canal functioned successfully through the rest of the 1800s, although its operations often were hindered by flood damage. Competition and high maintenance costs finally closed the C&O in 1924, and large sections were filled in to make way for other development. But much of the waterway through the Georgetown area was preserved as a public park.[64]

In addition to damaging the canal, Georgetown's seasonal floods, along with often oppressive winters, caused other major economic disruptions. Spring rains regularly sent destructive floodwaters swirling through the city's lower elevations, where most businesses were located. A fast-moving flood in June 1836 swamped the wharves and filled cellars with several feet of mud. Ruinous floods also plagued the city in April and September 1843. A rapid river surge in October 1847 carved away the banks of the canal in several places and left so much debris in the river that navigation was suspended until the spring of 1848, dealing a crippling blow to the shipping trade. An April 1852 flood submerged local bridges and halted navigation for the entire summer. The floods cost millions of dollars in infrastructure repair and lost business.

Frequent frigid winters also brought trouble. In the unusually cold January 1827, when a massive fire tore through Alexandria, Virginia, many citizens of Georgetown ice-skated down the river to help, pulling fire engines like giant sleds over the frozen stream. The winter of 1829–30 was so cold that the Potomac was frozen solid until spring floods broke the ice into massive chunks. The icebergs then rushed down the river with such force that they

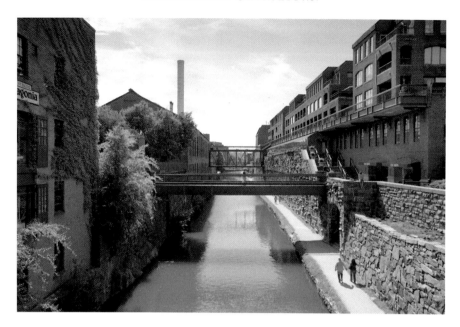

The remnants of the Chesapeake and Ohio Canal are a popular public park along the Potomac through Georgetown. *Photo by Missy Loewe.*

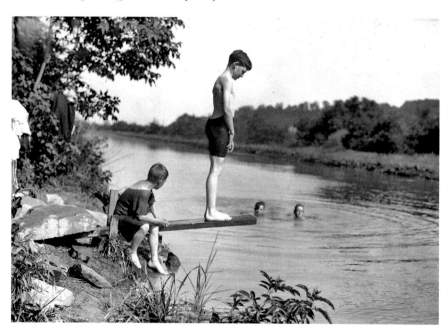

In addition to improving river transportation, the Chesapeake and Ohio Canal provided recreation for the Georgetown area. Youngsters take a summer dip in the channel about 1900. *National Photo Company Collection (reproduction number 19423). Courtesy Library of Congress, Prints and Photographs Division.*

ripped a large ship from the Georgetown docks and destroyed a bridge. Ice also closed the river in 1835, when January temperatures plummeted to sixteen degrees below zero, and in the winter of 1839–40, when an early spring thaw again battered local bridges with gigantic shards of ice.[65]

The bitter winters sometimes had benefits. Long periods of extreme cold reduced the next season's insect populations, which, although the medical profession did not yet realize it, helped control epidemics of mosquito-borne illnesses such as malaria and yellow fever. The bone-chilling freeze of 1840 proved to be the solution to another vexing bug problem. Ships often arrived at Georgetown loaded with large rocks that were used as ballast. To make room for the hogsheads of tobacco bound for Europe, the stones were unloaded and stacked along the shore and often were used to build houses and pave streets. One load of rocks from the West Indies contained a colony of stowaway ants that thrived in the warm humidity of the Georgetown summer and soon were crawling all over town.

"Chronicler" Jackson, who vividly remembered the plague of ants, wrote that the swarming insects "multiplied by thousands and millions, and entered into every store and dwelling, as they multiplied and marched onward due north." The vicious fire ants aggressively

> infested the walls of buildings, and concealed themselves in the cracks and openings. The chronicler has many times struck, with a stone, a brick or stone wall, when thousands would come to the surface and run in every direction. Their bite or sting was painful; and such a nuisance had they become to the property of the citizens, that our corporation offered a reward for their destruction by paying one dollar per quart for all dead ants brought to the office. After paying out several hundred dollars, the cold winter of 1840–41 set in, which completely destroyed them.[66]

High Society

Giving Away Fortunes and Brides

Since the Federal City was established in the late 1700s, Georgetown has been synonymous with high society in the nation's capital. The glittering galas and parties in its palatial homes, hosted and attended by leading luminaries of American culture, have become legendary.

Among the most highly visible figures in the Georgetown social circles were the town's mayors. Almost always, the mayors were wealthy captains of industry who used large and lavish social events to enhance their business and political connections. The city's longest-serving mayor, John Cox, certainly fit the description. During his term from 1822 until 1845, Cox hosted scores of dignitaries from across the nation and around the world, including one of America's most celebrated foreign visitors, the Marquis de Lafayette, whose U.S. tour in 1824 made national headlines.

Lafayette, a close colleague of George Washington, had been instrumental in winning the War for Independence. The renowned French military strategist, who came to America as a nineteen-year-old major general to aid the patriotic cause, became one of the most admired heroes of the Revolution before retuning home to France after the war.

In 1824, as the fiftieth anniversary of the Declaration of Independence approached, President James Monroe invited Lafayette back to the United States to join the celebration. The visit turned into a yearlong progression of jubilant public events, with Lafayette stopping in each of the twenty-four states of the union. He arrived first in New York, to tumultuous fanfare as his ship entered the harbor, and then made ceremonial appearances at

Revolutionary War sites in Boston, Philadelphia and other cities. He also spent time visiting and reminiscing with his old friends, former presidents Thomas Jefferson, James Madison and John Adams; future presidents John Quincy Adams, Andrew Jackson and William Henry Harrison; Secretary of State Henry Clay; and relatives of departed comrades George Washington and Alexander Hamilton.

During the District of Columbia leg of his tour, Lafayette made a solemn pilgrimage to George Washington's tomb at Mount Vernon, escorted by his friend George Washington Parke Custis. Custis—raised at Mount Vernon by his grandmother, Martha Washington, and the first president, who adopted him as a son—knew Lafayette from Revolutionary days. Lafayette also addressed Congress and was entertained at the White House and at several other grand homes, including the elegant mansions of Georgetown.

In addition to Mayor Cox, former Georgetown mayor Henry Foxhall and Thomas Peter, son of the town's first mayor, Robert Peter, also hosted Lafayette. Peter threw a huge party at his Tudor Place estate. His wife, another grandchild of Martha Washington who went by the nickname Patsy, also knew Lafayette from her childhood.

At Mayor Cox's reception, the public adulation for Lafayette was so intense that "one young lady in her enthusiasm fell upon her knees before the Marquis and impressed a kiss upon his hands," historian Grace Dunlop Ecker wrote, noting in her account of the elaborate evening that

> *there was a fashion in those days of decorating the floor by painting a pattern around the edges with colored chalks—garlands of roses entwined with the flags of the two countries. A marvelous supper was served; it is said it included 600 reed birds. It is to be hoped it also included other things more substantial than this high-sounding but sparsely covered game.*[67]

Cox also put his ornate horse-drawn coach and its driver at Lafayette's disposal during his Washington stay. The stylish French general got along famously with Cox, who was widely regarded as a dandy because of his expensive taste in housing, transportation, dining and clothes. Townsfolk at the time were known to marvel that "he would saunter down town in silk stockings and pumps, not getting a spot upon himself, while other men would be up to their ankles in mud, for in those days there were no pavements" on many of Georgetown's streets and walkways.

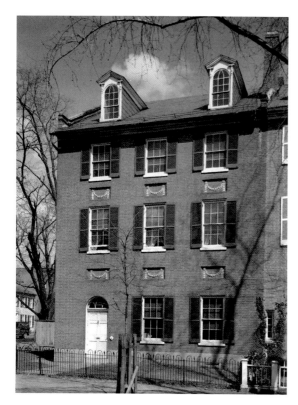

Left: Homes known as Cox's Row at 3327 N Street, owned by Georgetown's longest-serving mayor, John Cox. The house was the scene of an 1824 reception for the Marquis de Lafayette and other noteworthy social events. *John O. Brostrup, April 1937. HABS (reproduction number HABS DC, GEO, 37-1). Courtesy Library of Congress, Prints and Photographs Division.*

Below: The home of munitions manufacturer Henry Foxhall, a mayor of Georgetown who hosted General Lafayette and strictly enforced the city's "blue laws" to maintain the sanctity of the Sabbath. The home is at 3123 Dumbarton Street. *HABS (reproduction number HABS DC, GEO, 54-3). Courtesy Library of Congress, Prints and Photographs Division.*

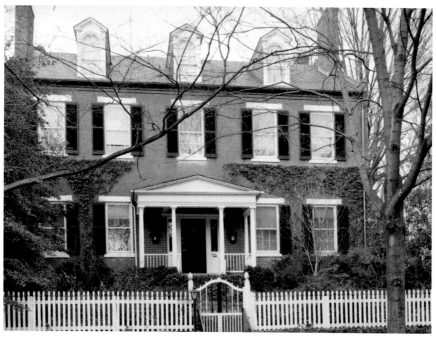

Foxhall, who served in city hall from 1819 until 1821, also hosted Lafayette in grand fashion. Years later, one of Foxhall's former slaves was well known for boasting about the time he drove General Lafayette in a carriage to the Foxhall home. Despite his career as wartime weapons manufacturer, Mayor Foxhall was known "as a real enthusiast in his religion" who strictly enforced Georgetown's "blue laws," which forbade certain commercial activities on Sundays. The laws against "profaning the Sabbath" had been on the books for many years, inherited from the original statutes drafted by the Maryland colony's Roman Catholic founders. The blue laws were punishable by fines or, in the case of disobedient slaves, public whippings.

Old-time residents remembered that

> *five dollars was the penalty for gaming, hunting and fishing on the Sabbath. No trading was allowed on the Lord's Day, except the selling of "fresh fish, milk, and other perishable goods." Cock-fighting and drinking, when indulged in by free men, were punished by a fine of $5.00, but when a slave was the offender, he received thirty-nine stripes on the bare back in a public place.*[68]

While religious dictum strictly regulated Sunday commerce, such stern standards apparently did not extend to the dress code for Georgetown's well-to-do youth, who often paraded about in less-than-modest attire. The six daughters of prominent banker John Marbury, for example, were singled out by local writer Grace Dunlop Ecker for

> *walking to and from school all winter wearing low-necked and short-sleeved dresses, covered only by a little cape. Not a case of poverty, I assure you, but of fashion! I was told this not long ago by a descendant, and of how they used to have to melt their gum shoes to get them on in cold weather.*[69]

The high-society Marbury sisters, like many of Georgetown's elite young ladies, attended school at "Miss English's Seminary for Young Ladies," a prestigious academy where the daughters of upscale families learned the proper social graces along with their classroom work. The seminary was founded in 1826 by an enterprising sixteen-year-old socialite who became disenchanted with living in her widowed father's home after his second marriage. Miss Lydia English launched her school with only three pupils, all girls from the neighborhood. But the youthful teacher's educational talents, marketing skills and personal charm soon earned the little institute a national reputation for quality and refinement.

"The school grew rapidly," local historian Sally Somervell Mackall wrote in the 1890s. "Girls from the highest social position came from all parts of the United States, many of their fathers being Senators and members of Congress." In addition to pupils from prominent families, Miss English hired well-heeled instructors, including the niece of Daniel Webster, a senator, secretary of state and three-time presidential candidate. Over the years, about eighteen hundred young ladies attended the seminary, which stood on the site of the original cabin built by early settler Ninian Beall.

"The school used to be the delight of the young men of the town, who worried poor Miss English very much, especially when she took the young ladies for a walk," Ms. Mackall wrote in her book *Early Days of Washington*.

> *Every year, on the first day of May, she would have a grand May festival and coronation of three queens and three kings. Each queen would be preceded by two little crown bearers and attended by 24 maids of honor.*
>
> *The whole town would be invited to these celebrations, and there would be speeches by prominent men, and a whole band furnished the music. In the evening there would be a grand ball in a room built for that purpose adjoining the school; later in the evening the guests would enjoy a handsome supper. It was astonishing what control Miss English exercised over the girls. The young ladies were required to write compositions at stated intervals.*
>
> *On one occasion, just before the close of the school for summer vacation, Jesse Benton* [daughter of the United States senator], *who was noted for being a troublesome girl and not for beauty, became impatient waiting for the teacher and wrote a piece of poetry, which I do not care to repeat, but which is still fresh in the memory of many of the old scholars. The poetry was very derogatory to Miss English and was reported by the teacher, which caused great disturbance, and although the young lady's "trunk was packed and in the hall, waiting for the porter's call," she was made to remain at the school a week longer.*

Ms. Mackall also described a "big, jolly, old-fashioned" lady known as "Aunt Abby" on Miss English's staff whose job was "to sit behind the parlor door when the young ladies had gentlemen friends visiting them." Aunt Abby was often seen

> *with lighted candle, running about the building at night to scare away the young men; but, notwithstanding their vigilance, occasionally a rope with a*

basket attached would be lowered from one of the third-story windows by the young ladies and filled with good things by the young men.

On the corner diagonally across from the school stood an old water pump, where the young men of the town were very fond of getting a drink, because they frequently saw the young ladies at the windows. One young man, who was very bashful but very fond of watching the girls, used to drink and drink. At last, it became quite a joke. One day the girls determined to see how long he would remain; they therefore took turns to watch, and the poor man pretended to be drinking the entire day.[70]

In addition to the seminary, a large contingent of art and dancing instructors catered to Georgetown's affluent residents. One local advertisement gave notice that "Mr. Carle, dancing master, may be spoke with on school days at Mrs. White's Tavern," and another encouraged customers to try the "Dancing School of J.B. Duclaviacq at his dancing room back of Mr. Turner's Counting House." Another ad told the town that

a night Dancing-School for the Reception of Gentlemen who are not at leisure to attend in the Day-time will be kept the evenings of the School days. The Price to each Scholar will be Four dollars. A subscription is lodged with Mr. Peter Casanave.[71]

A popular dancing venue in the later 1800s was a large Georgetown home where a widow lived with her "two pretty grown daughters who gave dancing lessons in their roomy basement on Friday afternoons, their mother supplying the music on a square piano, the only piece of furniture in the room," local writer Josephine Davis Leary recounted.

It used to seem to me that the old lady and the piano were a good deal alike: both showing signs of wear, both quite angular, both having thin voices, but both very nice to have around.

Perhaps the room had been converted from a cellar to a ballroom, I'm not sure, only as I remember it, the floor was the most rickety one I had ever known, rising and falling with the motion of the dancers. This was particularly true when Mary Polk danced, granddaughter of President Polk, a buxom girl whose "joie de vivre" was as exaggerated as her weight. We all loved to be her partner.[72]

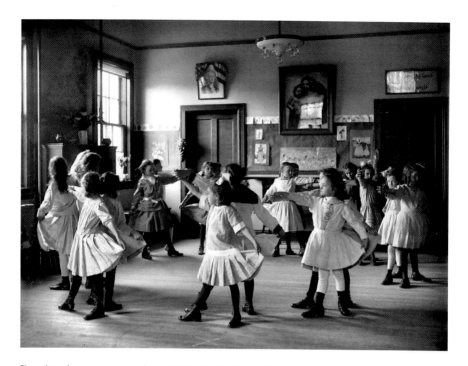

Dancing classes were popular activities for the little girls and young men and women of Georgetown. Students from William Lee's School practice their steps about 1900. *National Photo Company Collection (reproduction number 30742). Courtesy Library of Congress, Prints and Photographs Division.*

Cocktails and card playing also were cultural mainstays in Georgetown. "Gaming at cards at private balls and parties" and sipping a "toddy at dinner date back to the earliest knowledge of society in this vicinity," one resident recalled. "Card playing, horse-racing and other sports were fashionable and popular and had not abated in 1800 when the Government came." Britain's minister to America in 1805, Sir Augustus Foster, noted that the grand balls in Georgetown usually featured "cards for everybody, loo for the girls—brag for the men." Brag, called "the longest-standing British representative of the poker family," and loo, also called lanterloo, were favorite card games in the nineteenth century.[73]

Theatre performances were eagerly attended as well, with traveling troupes of actors presenting the latest plays in local auditoriums. Among the more fashionable venues for drama in the early 1800s was Mrs. Suter's Ballroom in Union Tavern.[74]

Portraiture also was popular in the 1800s, and affluent folks in Georgetown loved to have their pictures painted. A procession of well-known artists came

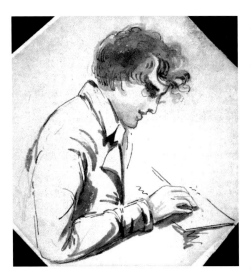

A self-portrait by famed portrait artist Gilbert Stuart (1755–1828), whose likenesses of George Washington and other early presidents are among the most famous works of art in American history. *Courtesy Library of Congress, Marian S. Carson Collection.*

through town looking for business. Legendary painter Gilbert Stuart, whose full-length likeness of George Washington survived the War of 1812 to adorn the East Room of the White House, set up shop in Georgetown for two years beginning in 1803. His work still graces homes and museums in Georgetown, Alexandria and Washington. Stuart's subjects included Thomas Jefferson and every other U.S. president through John Quincy Adams. Known as an outgoing and engaging fellow who became a fixture of society while in Georgetown, Stuart also logged many hours at Mount Vernon, painting General Washington and members of his family. Of all the famous people who posed for the renowned artist, it was said that George Washington was the only person in whose presence Stuart was ever embarrassed.[75]

Among the hundreds of fabled social events in Georgetown's history, perhaps the most memorable was the unlikely wedding of a dumpy, middle-aged Russian diplomat and a stunningly pretty teenage schoolgirl from one of the town's old-line families. Several accounts of the extravagant marriage ceremony about 1840 have been reported, but the most colorful version comes from the 1899 book *Early Days of Washington*, whose author, Sally Somervell Mackall, was certain that

> *many of the readers will be interested in the marriage of the Russian Minister, M. de Bodisco, to Harriet Beall Williams, daughter of Brooke Williams, Sr. (of good old Revolutionary stock), the most brilliant wedding that has ever taken place in the District.*
>
> *In former days, the foreign ministers preferred living in Georgetown, and did so until their governments required their representatives to reside in the Capital. When Mr. Bodisco first came to Georgetown to live, he gave a Christmas party to his nephews Waldamer and Boras Bodisco. To*

this party all the boys and girls of the town were bidden; great bonfires lighted the way, for there was no gas in those days. Enchanting strains of music, flowers and lights were everywhere, and very happy was every boy and girl present.

Among the guests was the beautiful Harriet Beall Williams, whom Mr. Bodisco saw there for the first time. Her charms completely fascinated the old gentleman; the morning after the ball he walked up the hill to meet her and escorted her to school. Thus started a love story that ended in a happy marriage, notwithstanding the disparagement of age. The bride was only sixteen and considered the beauty of America. (Indeed the entire Williams family were strikingly handsome.) Mr. Bodisco was about fifty years of age. Her family were much opposed to the marriage, and at one time the engagement came near being broken. She told Mr. Bodisco that her grandmother and everybody else thought he was entirely too old and ugly. Mr. Bodisco's reply was that she might find some one younger and better looking, but no one that would love her more than he did.

The pudgy envoy from Moscow and the lovely young student from Miss English's Seminary were married on a June afternoon at the bride's family home on Georgetown Heights. Because Miss Williams's father was not living, "her hand was given in marriage" by a close family friend, Kentucky senator and former secretary of state Henry Clay. The ceremony was followed by "a brilliant reception."

Ms. Mackall offered a vivid description of the bridal attire:

Her trousseau came from abroad, and her bridal robe was a marvel of rich white satin and costly lace, which fell in graceful folds around her; the low-cut dress showed to perfection her lovely white shoulders and neck. On her fair brow and golden hair was worn a coronet of rarest pearls, the gift of the groom. The effect was wonderfully brilliant.

Groom Alexander de Bodisco, also splendidly attired for the nuptial, "wore his court dress of velvet and lace."

"All the bridesmaids, seven in number, were beautiful girls about her own age," Ms. Mackall wrote. "Their gowns were figured white satin, cut low in the neck with short sleeves, and trimmed with blond lace." The groomsmen reportedly included President Martin van Buren, fellow senator and former U.S. ambassador to Russia James Buchanan, who later became president, and the ministers from Britain, Austria and the Netherlands.

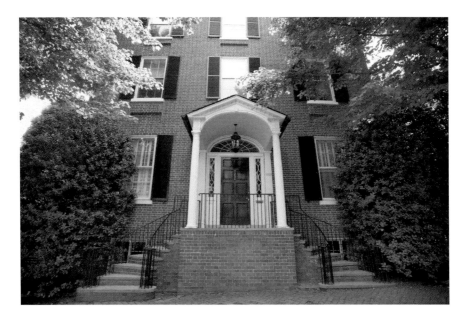

The home of Russian diplomat Alexander de Bodisco, whose marriage to Georgetown schoolgirl Harriett Beall Williams was the most memorable wedding in the town's history. The house at 3322 O Street was the scene of numerous noteworthy social events. *Photo by Missy Loewe.*

"The house and grounds were thronged with noted guests, strolling amid sweet-scented flowers and lemon trees hanging with rich golden fruit," Ms. Mackall wrote. "The brilliant array of guests, the sparkling eyes and bright smiles of beautiful belles, formed a fairy scene, long to be remembered." The event was followed by other balls and receptions around town, and a few days later, "President Van Buren gave a handsome dinner at the White House in honor of Madame Bodisco."[76]

In addition to lavish lifestyles, Georgetown's high society also was characterized by an unprecedented sense of philanthropy. The town's wealthy elite became pioneers in demonstrating how those who amass great riches can "give back to the community." Some of America's earliest philanthropists were the bankers and merchants of Georgetown, whose civic involvement and fabulous generosity were instrumental in elevating the town's educational facilities, charitable causes, religious institutions and overall beauty and quality of life.

Wealthy hardware merchant Edward Magruder Linthicum, who opened his first business in Georgetown in 1819, was a trustee of the Methodist Church and a member of the town council who became one of the city's first and most generous benefactors. Linthicum was described as "a prominent and prosperous merchant of the highest type, a man of great civic activities, and deeply interested in everything which tended to beautify the community." The "very imposing looking gentleman" provided large endowments to churches, schools and charities. For many years, the school he funded, named the Linthicum Institute in his honor, was one of the town's best-known centers of education.

Another benevolent civic leader was Massachusetts native George Peabody, who was born in 1795 and came to Georgetown as a young orphan to work for his uncle. At age seventeen, Peabody volunteered to serve in the War of 1812. After the war, when he was about nineteen, he became a partner in a dry goods store with another Georgetown resident, Elisha Riggs. The enterprise thrived and expanded into other business areas, and by 1830, it had grown into one of the largest merchant and banking companies in the nation. A few years later, Peabody moved to London to set up a trading and banking corporation, which became one of the most successful in the world during the 1840s. Later, he went into business with renowned banker J.P. Morgan.

Peabody, who called himself a "confirmed old bachelor," contributed vast sums to charity in England and the United States. His numerous gifts included money to establish Georgetown's first public library, an early expedition to explore the Arctic, museums in London and his native Massachusetts and colleges and universities in the American South. His name is affixed to many civic institutions that benefited from his gifts, and some have called him the "father of modern philanthropy." British statesman William Ewart Gladstone said of his friend George Peabody, "He taught the world how a man may be master of his fortune, and not its slave."[77]

The most revered of Georgetown's great philanthropists was William Wilson Corcoran, the third son of four-time mayor Thomas Corcoran, born in 1798. Contrary to his father's wishes that he pursue a classical education, young Corcoran, after a short stint as a day student at Georgetown College, went to work at age seventeen in a dry goods store belonging to his brothers, James and Thomas. Two years later, they set him up in a small store of his own, and two years after that, they started a wholesale auction and commission business. The Corcoran brothers fared well until a recession in the 1820s, when their business joined many others in bankruptcy. They settled with their creditors for fifty cents on the dollar. But William Corcoran started over and rebuilt his fortune. Twenty-four years later—in a gesture that stunned his former creditors, bolstered his community esteem and ignited his fame as a philanthropist—he repaid every person's losses plus interest.

Corcoran built his corporate comeback on banking and finance. He became an officer at Georgetown's Bank of Columbia, and then he operated a brokerage business in downtown Washington in partnership with another Georgetown banker, George W. Riggs. Riggs's brother, Elisha, an early business partner of fellow philanthropist George Peabody, also joined the firm, which was called Corcoran and Riggs. They bought out another Washington bank in 1845 to form the Riggs National Bank, which for decades was one of the strongest financial institutions in America.

Corcoran's rare marketing skills were heralded in 1848, when he went on an overseas mission to sell U.S. government bonds. Amid overwhelming predictions that he would fail, given the fact that no securities from the American treasury had sold abroad in more than a decade, Corcoran struck up a partnership with Thomas Baring of London's venerable Baring Brothers banking firm. In record time, Corcoran and the Baring Brothers sold out the entire $5 million bond offering, a huge financial achievement in the 1840s. Delighted with the performance, U.S. officials awarded the firm of Corcoran and Riggs a large chunk of the government's financial business for years to come, helping Corcoran build enormous wealth.

In April 1854, Corcoran retired from the firm, saying that he had made more than enough money, and he spent the next forty-five years of his life, until his death at age ninety-four, giving away his riches "in a manner unknown before that time." Corcoran's community contributions began with a fund to buy firewood and other provisions for the poor and escalated into endowments for parks, schools, churches, art galleries and museums in Georgetown, Washington and other cities around the nation.

"The business of his life then was judiciously giving away his money," Ms. Ecker wrote.

> Here are some of the ways he did it: colleges had always appealed to him, and he was for many years Rector of Columbian University in Washington, now renamed George Washington, and gave freely to it. His name is now borne by one of their largest and best buildings, Corcoran Hall. He gave to the Maryland Agricultural College, to the College of William and Mary in Virginia, loaned money to the Virginia Military Institute and when the bonds came due, tore them up—a little way he had.
>
> To Washington and Lee University, also in Lexington, he gave $20,000 besides the library. His portrait hangs in the little chapel in Lexington where

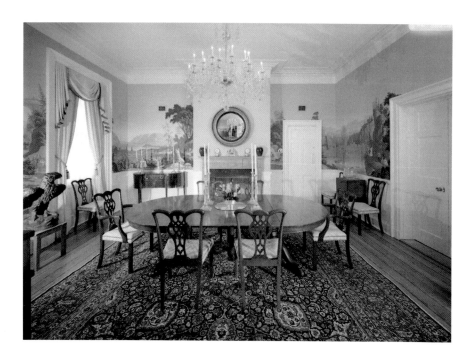

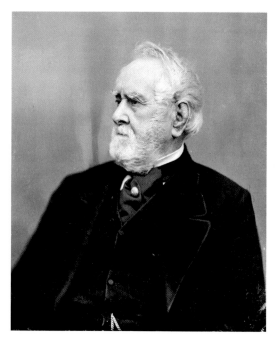

Above: The dining room of the Riggs-Riley House at 3038 N Street, a home of Georgetown's famous Riggs banking family, who operated one of the most successful financial institutions in America. *HABS (reproduction number HABS DC, GEO, 48-7). Courtesy Library of Congress, Prints and Photographs Division.*

Left: William Wilson Corcoran (1798–1888), the renowned philanthropist whose many gifts to the community included Oak Hill Cemetery and the Corcoran Gallery of Art. *Courtesy Library of Congress, Prints and Photographs Division, Brady-Handy Collection.*

lies the body of his friend, Robert E. Lee. To the University of Virginia he gave $100,000 which endowed two chairs, also giving $5,000 to resuscitate the library which had suffered during the war and the period following, from being unable to procure any new books. He was one of the first people to subscribe to the fund being raised by certain ladies to purchase Mount Vernon, after the Washington family found themselves unable to keep it up, and offered it to the United States Government, which refused to buy and preserve it.

Stories of Corcoran's generosity abound, including recollections of him strolling the streets of Georgetown, handing out cash to unemployed workers and, while on a tour of the South following the Civil War, writing so many checks to help rebuild battle-damaged towns that his staff had trouble keeping up with the accounting. When funds were lacking to resume construction of the Washington Monument, which had been halted before the Civil War, Corcoran organized a huge benefit to help raise the money needed to finish the project. When completed in 1884, it was the tallest structure in the world. Once, during a boat ride, Corcoran's ten-year-old daughter fell overboard and a passenger named Gordon Smith jumped in the water to rescue her. Corcoran rewarded the man with $1,000—considered a fortune back then—and offered him a job.

In addition to being an eminent philanthropist, Corcoran was remembered in Georgetown as an avid card player. He "always loved to play whist, and in the last years of his life his nephews and nieces and great-nephews and great-nieces used to go often to play with him and pass the long evenings," Ms. Ecker reported. "A friend of mine remembers being taken as a little girl, with her grandmother, to call on him. She was fascinated by the room where he sat," and youngsters so enjoyed the old gentleman's company that they were "distressed when told to go out in the garden to play."

Perhaps Corcoran's best-remembered contributions to the Washington area are the grand Corcoran Gallery of Art near the White House and Georgetown's Oak Hill Cemetery, for which he donated the land in 1849 and where he was buried in February 1888. Ms. Ecker, who watched Corcoran's long funeral procession wind its way toward the graveyard, wrote:

I remember as a little girl standing at the window of my home facing 31st Street and hearing the bell of near-by Christ Church toll ninety strokes as carriage after carriage passed slowly up the hill. My brother and I counted them, and there were ninety-nine.[78]

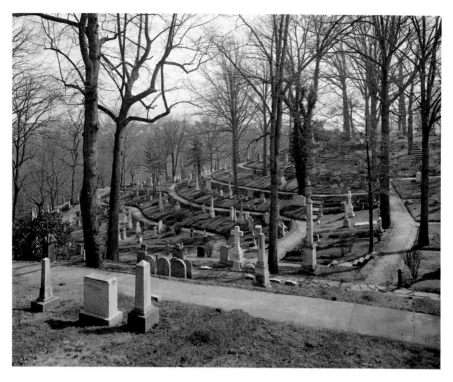

Oak Hill Cemetery, final resting place for many of the town's most notable people, including W.W. Corcoran, who donated land for the graveyard. The tree-shaded cemetery slopes from the Heights of Georgetown to Rock Creek. *National Photo Company Collection (reproduction number 33611). Courtesy Library of Congress, Prints and Photographs Division.*

Oak Hill, covering several forested acres descending from Georgetown Heights to Rock Creek, is the final resting place for hundreds of prominent people in the history of the nation's capital. "To me," Mrs. Ecker wrote,

> *no other cemetery that I have ever seen in this country or abroad has the same natural beauty of slopes and trees—in the spring bedecked like a bride in flowering white shrubs; in the fall its towering oak trees aflame with shades of crimson.*[79]

Carved into the lavish monuments and imposing mausoleums are names of citizens from the earliest days of Georgetown, including philanthropist Edward Linthicum, longtime religious leader Stephen Bloomer Balch and Revolutionary War general Uriah Forrest. The graveyard also holds the remains of Russian ambassador Alexander de Bodisco; Tennessee senator John Eaton, who was secretary of war under President Andrew Jackson; prominent attorney Philip Barton Key, uncle of Francis Scott Key; Edwin Stanton, President Lincoln's secretary of war; and dozens of other noteworthy Georgetown and Washington residents, including Supreme Court justice Edward Douglas White, Secretary of State Dean Acheson of the Truman administration and *Washington Post* publishers Philip and Katherine Graham, who lived just across the street from the cemetery's main gate. The names on the tombstones, along with the beauty of the place, have made Oak Hill a popular stop for tourists. Georgetown's main cemetery, like the town itself, has become a symbol of tasteful style and high society in the nation's capital.

"A great deal of fashion has come to Georgetown," Ms. Ecker wrote,

> *as in the early days of the bringing of the government when Washington City was a waste and almost entirely one big mud puddle, and the foreign ministers and many high in our government sought the comfort and dignity of this town, which was then far from young. Again in later years there has been an exodus across Rock Creek of men and women high in the government; in the diplomatic corps; in industry; in literature and the arts.*[80]

For Sale: Family of Five

Slavery and Civil War

Since the early days of the tobacco trade, slavery had been a part of life in Georgetown. The tobacco growers needed large numbers of field hands to plow, plant, cultivate, harvest, haul and process the labor-intensive crop that brought wealth to the Chesapeake region. In addition to toiling in the tobacco fields and working as household servants in Georgetown's affluent homes, slave labor also helped build the new city of Washington, including the Capitol and the White House. Despite some strong opposition to the buying and selling of human beings, slavery, as the backbone of the tobacco economy, was politically and socially accepted from colonial times until the mid-1800s. Georgetown historically had a large African population, including slaves and free blacks, many of whom had earned or purchased their freedom.

Slave trading in Georgetown dated back to at least 1760, when merchant John Beattie established a slave market near the waterfront. It was a thriving business that earned him a sizable fortune over the years. Other slave markets, also called "slave pens," operated in Georgetown, including one at McCandless's Tavern near the intersection of present-day M Street and Wisconsin Avenue. In addition to regular auctions at the markets, slaves were also acquired through inheritance and private transactions. Estate sales, for example, often included slaves as part of the merchandise.

A July 8, 1834 advertisement in the *National Intelligencer* newspaper announced, "Stock, Slaves, Furniture, etc., at Auction, by Thomas C. Wright, Georgetown." The ad told potential buyers that

National Intelligencer.

WASHINGTON: TUESDAY, MARCH 27, 1832.

FORTY DOLLARS REWARD.

RANAWAY from the subscriber, living near Notting-ham, Prince George's county, on the morning of the 23d instant, Negro man LONDON, aged about thir-ty-six years, down look when spoken to, middle size, ra-ther an ill looking fellow. He has relations at Dr. Ber-ry's, near the Eastern Branch Bridge, where he will pro-bably go, or possibly to the City of Washington. The above reward will be paid, if delivered to me, or secured in any jail, so that I get him again.

mar 27—w4w   WILLIAM B. CHEW.

NEGROES FOR SALE.

A FAMILY of most likely, healthy, and valuable NEGROES, consisting of two women, about thir-ty to fifty years old, one of them has a young child. Five, males from 12 to 28 years old, some of them good house servants. These negroes were the proper-ty of the late Captain James Hoban, who has directed, by his will, that they shall not be sold or taken out of the District of Columbia.

Persons disposed to purchase will be pleased to apply to either

JAMES HOBAN,
THOS. CARBERY, } Executors of
march 27—dtf   JAS. HOBAN.

Slavery was a popular topic for newspaper advertisements in the 1800s. *The* National Intelligencer, *Tuesday, March 27, 1832.*

on Wednesday next, the 15th, if fair (if otherwise, on Friday the 17th) at 9 o'clock a.m. at the residence of the late Col. Edmund Brooke, deceased, above the Foundry near Georgetown, all the personal estate of said deceased, consisting of all the Household and Kitchen furniture, 5 Feather Beds, 3 Mattresses, Bedsteads and Bedding, Sideboard, Silver Spoons, Ladle, etc. Also 2 Horses, 2 Milk cows, a large lot of Farming Utensils of every description. Also, without reserve or restriction, eight valuable Slaves: 2 Young Men, 1 Valuable female House-servant, an excellent Cook, and her five children, all uncommonly likely. Terms, cash before delivery.[81]

Sometimes blacks were sold off as an entire family. A *National Intelligencer* ad from March 27, 1832, announced:

NEGROES FOR SALE: A family of most likely, healthy, and valuable NEGROES, consisting of two women, about 30 to 50 years old, one of them has a young child. Five males, from 12 to 28 years old, some of them good house servants. These negroes were the property of the late Captain James Hoban , who has directed, by his will, that they shall not be sold or taken out of the District of Columbia. Persons disposed to purchase will be pleased to apply to either JAMES HOBAN or THOS. CARBERY, executors of Jas. Hoban.

Hoban, who died in 1831, was the Irish-born architect of the White House who used slave labor in building the presidential residence. The executor, by the same name, was his son, a lawyer who worked in Washington and Georgetown.

The blacks in Georgetown, both slave and free, often encountered harsher laws and restrictions than the whites, resulting in widespread racial segregation and discrimination. Blacks were subject to nighttime curfews and prohibitions against assembling in large groups. Most schools taught only white children, and many business establishments and churches banned blacks or relegated them to certain areas. Some churches confined blacks to the balcony and installed separate stairs for them outside the building. Many laws were intended to prevent black uprisings as antislavery rhetoric grew more heated during the 1800s and as Georgetown's African population increased. The 1800 census reported that the town's 5,120 residents included 227 free blacks and 1,449 slaves.

Slavery also was governed by state statutes, often patterned after the slave codes developed in the 1600s by English colonists on Caribbean sugar plantations. The laws often made slavery a permanent condition, inherited through the mother, and classified slaves as property, similar to real estate. Being property, slaves could not own property or enter contracts, which sometimes included marriage.

Often, slaves would escape, with owners offering rewards for their capture. Newspaper classified sections commonly contained ads with bounties for runaways, such as a March 27, 1832,notice in the *National Intelligencer* that read:

> *FORTY DOLLARS REWARD: Runaway, from the subscriber, living near Nottingham, Prince Georges county, on the morning of the 23d instant, Negro man LONDON, aged about thirty-six years, down look when spoken to, middle size, rather an ill looking fellow. He has relations at Dr. Berry's near the Eastern Branch Bridge, where he will probably go, or possibly to the City of Washington. The above reward will be paid, if delivered to me, or secured in any jail, so that I get him again. WILLIAM B. CHEW.*

But despite the restrictions and cruel conditions of captivity, the life of a slave in the District of Columbia was far easier than in many southern states, where subjugated blacks were forced to toil in the scorching heat of rice and cotton fields. Many southern slaves were denied schooling, housed in cramped cabins resembling livestock stalls, strictly forbidden to engage in any activity beyond their assigned duties and disciplined with stinging lashes from a whip. In the District, slaves could hire out their services and could live apart from their masters. Free blacks could own property, run their own businesses and operate schools. The more lenient treatment inspired free blacks to migrate to the area. By 1860, the population of the District of Columbia, which included Georgetown, was about 75 percent black, with 11,131 free blacks and 3,185 slaves.[82]

As the years progressed, public angst over slavery became more intense, and the national capital area—with its large black population, strong presence of foreign diplomats and visitors and intense media coverage— became a focal point of the debate. More and more people began decrying the hypocrisy of slavery in light of the nation's founding principles of human equality. Two strong abolitionist societies had formed in the District by the 1820s, and in 1828, more than one thousand residents signed a petition calling on Congress to outlaw slave trading. Newspapers took sides in the debate, and impassioned arguments dominated the press, as well as public gatherings and legislative sessions.

Crusading organizations such as New York's American Anti-Slavery Society launched high-profile campaigns aimed at Washington. The New York group published a widely distributed poster in 1836 demanding an end to slavery in the nation's capital. The document, headlined "Slave Market of America," opened with biblical passages condemning oppression, followed by quotations from the Declaration of Independence and the U.S. Constitution on liberty and equality. The wordy, picture-laden placard then outlined legal grounds for abolishing slavery in America's capital and listed the names of proslavery congressmen.[83]

The black community monitored the debate closely. In 1848, a group of slaves in Georgetown and Washington was sufficiently emboldened by the rising rhetoric to take part in a daring dash for freedom that became one of the most famous slave escape attempts in American history. It began with several days of quiet planning by local activists to draw national attention to the abolitionist cause by liberating slaves from the District of Columbia and carrying them by boat to free states in the North. The planners worked with the local chapter of the Underground Railroad, a clandestine network that secretly ferried blacks away from oppression in the South. In the Washington area, the Underground Railroad's hiding places included a vault in the cemetery of the Mt. Zion Methodist Episcopal Church in Georgetown. The crypt was used to store bodies during the winter when the ground was too frozen for grave digging.

The organizers included Paul Jennings, the black butler of Senator Daniel Webster who also had been a servant in James Madison's White House. Webster had purchased Jennings's freedom for $120, and Jennings was continuing to work for him while repaying the sum in $8 monthly installments. Other organizers were a free black named Daniel Bell and a slave named Samuel Edmonson, who booked several of his relatives on the escape boat. White abolitionist Daniel Drayton and the ship's white owner and captain, Edward Sayres, were paid by the organizers to lead the expedition.

On the drizzly night of April 15, 1848, small groups of slaves crept from their quarters and made their way quietly through a light fog to Washington's Seventh Street Wharf. Waiting at the dock was their ride to freedom—a two-masted sailing ship called the *Pearl*. The runaways, who included children and elderly members of several families, were mostly workers in hotels and wealthy homes. One escapee was owned by former first lady Dolley Madison and several worked in the homes of leading Georgetown citizens, including the family of tobacco shipper Francis Dodge.

Drayton and Sayres planned to leave under cover of darkness and travel more than one hundred miles to the mouth of the Potomac, another one hundred miles across the Chesapeake Bay and then up the Delaware River to the free state of New Jersey. The schooner's cargo of human contraband consisted of thirty-eight men, twenty-six women and thirteen children—the largest group of slaves in U.S. history to attempt a mass escape. With all seventy-seven passengers onboard, the *Pearl* slipped quietly from the dock sometime after midnight and headed downriver. It was slow going at first, with little wind to propel the craft. By daybreak, the *Pearl* had drifted only as far as Alexandria. But with sunrise came stronger breezes, so the crew raised the sails and picked up speed.

About that time, the wealthy Dodges and other families in Georgetown and Washington were awakening to discover cold, empty kitchens with no slaves preparing their Sunday breakfast. Stunned households in Georgetown hastily checked with their neighbors and realized that a major escape had taken place. Word spread through the morning church services, and search parties began scouring the roads out of town when someone tipped the authorities that a large group of slaves had stolen away during the night on a boat down the Potomac.

The Dodge family immediately volunteered their steamboat, called the *Salem*, as a chase vehicle and organized a posse of police officers and slave owners to hunt down the escapees. The *Salem*, a much faster vessel than the *Pearl*, plowed southward down the Potomac, but its crew saw no sign of the missing slaves. The searchers were about to give up and turn back when a lookout spied the *Pearl* anchored in a shadowy cove near the mouth of the Potomac, where Sayres had stopped to wait for better weather before venturing out to the open waters of the bay.

The *Salem* abruptly veered into the cove, emitting a shrill-sounding jet of steam that alerted the fugitives that they had been discovered. As the steamboat chugged closer, the horrified slaves huddled with Drayton and Sayres and began debating whether to surrender or fight. As the *Salem* pulled alongside the *Pearl*, the slaves saw the heavily armed search party, realized they were outgunned and decided to give up peacefully. The *Salem* towed the *Pearl* back to Washington, where an impatient and angry crowd awaited. The prisoners spent the long ride bound and crammed into the ship's clammy cargo hold, anxiously pondering their fate.

The horde that lined the wharf cheered and jeered as the disheartened captives, heads hanging and arms tied behind their backs, were led off the ship. The whites in the ill-humored throng unleashed their loudest and most scathing taunts at the handcuffed Drayton and Sayres. Black onlookers stood farther away and stared solemnly, many with tears streaming down their cheeks. A newspaper reporter covering the arrival wrote, "The colored population are in anguish. They know that the runaways will be separated from friends and kindred and scattered over the land to see each other's faces no more." One mother of a *Pearl* passenger collapsed in sobs as her son emerged from the boat, wailing that he would be taken away from her forever.

A few slaves from the *Pearl* rejoined their owners, but most were handed over by their irate masters to traders who sold them south. Drayton and Sayres were jailed on charges of theft and transporting runaway slaves. While the escape failed, the organizers achieved their goal of attracting national attention. The incident made headlines across the country. Slaveholders in the Washington area were so inflamed that a large mob trooped to the downtown offices of an abolitionist newspaper called the *National Era*, whose editor many blamed for inspiring slave rebellions, and demanded that its printing presses be removed. Furious protesters marched on the newspaper office for several days in a series of violent confrontations that become known as the Washington Riots. The demonstrations ended only after the *National Era*'s office and editor received heavy police protection.

The local turmoil also was reflected in Congress, where Representative Joshua Giddings of Ohio introduced a resolution in the House. The resolution asked why, in the light of the popular struggles for freedom that were going on in Europe at the time, the *Pearl* fugitives were being jailed for seeking the rights of life, liberty and the pursuit of happiness cited in

America's Declaration of Independence. Representative Isaac Holmes of South Carolina led the proslavery side of the divisive argument, which finally ended when a slim majority of congressmen, including new Republican representative Abraham Lincoln of Illinois, voted to close debate.

Drayton and Sayres went on trial in July. Their prosecutor was Georgetown district attorney Barton Key, son of Francis Scott Key. They were defended by famed educator Horace Mann, who had come to Washington to fill the congressional seat of former president John Quincy Adams. Both suspects were cleared of the theft charges, but they were convicted of transporting runaway slaves and were assessed $10,000 in fines and court costs. Unable to pay, the men spent four years in prison until President Millard Fillmore granted them a pardon.[84]

Many historians and political scientists believe that the *Pearl* affair and the protests that followed it significantly strengthened the antislavery cause. The *National Era*, despite the attacks and threats, continued publishing and, in 1852, printed a series of articles by abolitionist writer Harriet Beecher Stowe that became the classic antislavery book *Uncle Tom's Cabin*. Slave-owning territories such as Maryland, Delaware and the District of Columbia made it illegal for any slave or free black to possess the book or any other abolitionist reading material.

A key milestone in the congressional slavery debate was the Compromise of 1850, a hotly contested decision over whether new territories joining the United States should allow slavery. The issue continued to intensify over the next ten years, and by 1860, many feared that the United States would be torn apart by the regional disagreements over slavery. When antislavery candidate Abraham Lincoln was elected to succeed President James Buchanan, secession of southern states seemed inevitable. In December 1860, shortly after Lincoln's victory, the legislature of South Carolina voted to leave the Union, followed shortly by other states in the South. When Lincoln took office, the nation was preparing for civil war. Just a few weeks after his inauguration on March 4, 1861, hostilities began when rebel forces fired on U.S. troops at Fort Sumter near Charleston, South Carolina. Lincoln declared the incident an act of war by the breakaway Confederate States of America, and the Civil War was underway. Virginia joined the Confederacy five days later.

The preparations for conflict had a profound effect on Washington and Georgetown. Several businesses shifted from their daily activities to begin working for the war effort. The Duvall Foundry, a metal works on the waterfront, revamped its operations to produce muskets for the Union side, while shipping firms began receiving supplies and equipment for the

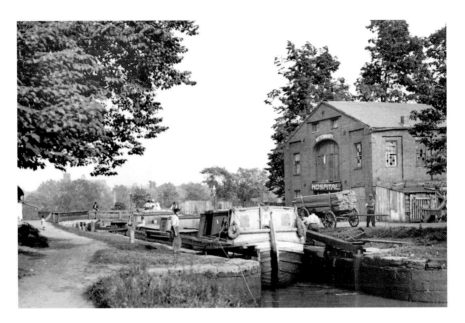

The Duvall Foundry at 1050 Thirtieth Street shifted its metalworking operations in 1861 to the production of muskets and other armaments for the Union side in the Civil War. *Courtesy Library of Congress.*

U.S. Army. Friends and family members found themselves on opposing sides, severing longtime alliances and prompting suspicion and hostilities among people in business, government and the military. Many residents of Georgetown signed up to fight for the Union, but many others sided with the South. Philanthropist W.W. Corcoran, known to be a Southern sympathizer, left the country until the war was over.

The District of Columbia, because of its proximity to Confederate lines, became a staging ground for the Union side, with troops arriving from across the Northern states to organize for battle. The war preparations quickly spilled into neighboring Georgetown. Early in 1861, several volunteer military units, including the Sixty-ninth New York and the Seventy-ninth Pennsylvania Regiments, arrived in the capital and were dispatched to Georgetown to await their combat assignments. The soldiers took over the campus of Georgetown College, whose buildings were converted into barracks and hospital facilities. The Seventy-ninth Pennsylvania Regiment, led by a bagpipe band and clad in their distinctive Scottish kilts, likely felt at home amid Georgetown's Scottish descendants. The college students showed their sympathies by wearing large lapel pins on their jackets: tricolor for the Union and blue for the Confederacy.[85]

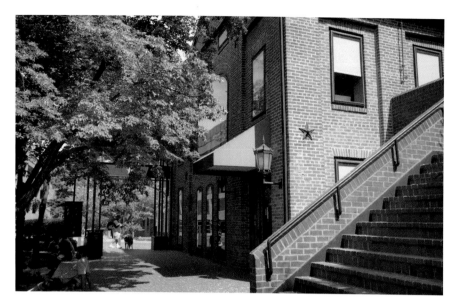

The Duvall Foundry today, converted into office space. *Photo by Missy Loewe.*

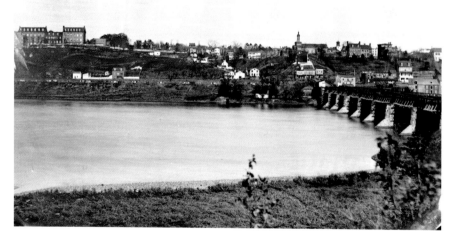

The Aqueduct Bridge between Georgetown and Virginia. During the Civil War, the Union army installed a roadbed of wooden boards that could be removed each evening to keep the Confederates from crossing into the Washington area. *William Morris Smith, November 11, 1865. Courtesy Library of Congress.*

Georgetown resident J. Holdsworth Gordon, a Southern-leaning student, later wrote:

> We boys fraternized with the soldiers, to a certain extent, many of whom were fine fellows and loved to talk with "the little Rebs" as some of us were dubbed. Indeed, these poor fellows, many of them almost boys just from home and home surroundings, were glad enough to find anyone with whom they might pass a word of friendship and fellowship. As we would see the sick and wounded brought in, our hearts could but go out to them in their suffering, and make us very anxious for the loved one away from us, who might at any moment be in their condition, and not under such favorable surroundings.[86]

As the war got underway, a top priority was keeping combat away from the Union capital. U.S. forces took control of Alexandria and the Virginia side of the Potomac across from Washington and Georgetown as a buffer against Confederate attack. On the high hill in Virginia that overlooked Georgetown, Union forces seized the columned mansion called Arlington House, which had been the home of General Robert E. Lee until he abandoned the property to command the Confederate army. The bridge connecting Georgetown to Virginia became a prime passage for troops and equipment between Washington and the combat zones. The army constructed a removable roadbed of wooden planks across the span, which could be dismantled each night to prevent Confederate forces from sneaking into town.[87]

The first major skirmish in the vicinity of Washington was the Battle of Bull Run near Manassas, Virginia, in July 1861. The engagement proved to be a good spectator draw, with streams of carriages from Georgetown and Washington crossing the Potomac to watch the fighting from nearby hilltops. It was a stunning defeat for the Union. Washington resident Rose O'Neal Greenhow, who lived near the White House and was later accused of being a Confederate spy, wrote a letter describing the city in the aftermath of Bull Run:

> In the world's history such a sight was never witnessed. Statesmen, senators, congressmen, generals and officers of every grade, soldiers, teamsters—all rushing in frantic flight, as if pursued by countless demons. For miles, the country was thick with ambulances, accoutrements of war, etc. The news of the disastrous rout of the Yankee army was cried through the streets…For days the wildest disorder reigned in the Capital. The streets of Washington were filled with stragglers, telling the doleful tale.[88]

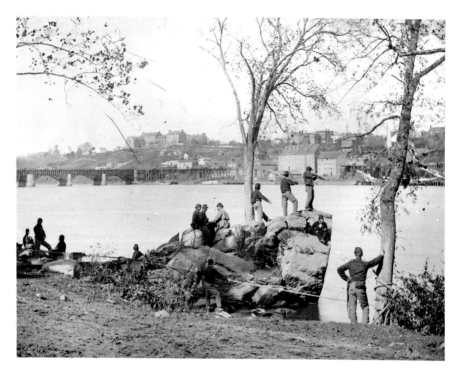

Civil War soldiers, some with rifles, look across the Potomac at Georgetown, with the Aqueduct Bridge in the background. *George Barnard, 1861. Courtesy Library of Congress, Civil War Glass Negative Collection.*

Being the U.S. cities closest to enemy lines, Washington and Georgetown were major receiving stations for the wounded. To help treat the injured soldiers, volunteers from across the North flocked to the Washington area. They included well-known poet Walt Whitman and novelist Louisa May Alcott, who helped staff medical facilities in Georgetown. As Union wounded were carted back across the Potomac from Bull Run and other battles, several buildings, including Miss Lydia English's Seminary for Young Women, were transformed into military hospitals.[89]

In addition to the college and seminary, other Georgetown buildings also were converted to wartime use. The Peter family, descendants of the town's first mayor, opened their Tudor Place mansion as a boardinghouse for Union officers. Family members said that they took in the military leaders to keep the house from being confiscated by the government for some other use.[90]

As the conflict raged on for the next four years, the soldiers and civilian volunteers who swelled the populations of Washington and Georgetown were joined by hundreds, and then thousands, of black refugees from the

South. Some signed up to fight for the Union but initially were turned down because the Militia Act of 1792, which governed army recruiting, allowed only "free white males" to serve. By 1862, however, the need for soldiers was sufficient for Union officials to waive the restriction. Soon, there were 166 all-black regiments in the Union army.

Many of the blacks who came to Washington settled in makeshift encampments throughout the area. The largest black enclave in Georgetown was the Herring Hill neighborhood, along Rock Creek near present-day P Street. Some speculate that the area derived its name from the fish that residents caught in the creek. Historian Mary Mitchell wrote in her book *Chronicles of Georgetown Life, 1865–1900* that "free Negroes had developed a stable and self-sustaining community of 951 persons by 1860" in Herring Hill, which grew many times larger as the war continued.

Wisps of smoke from little cook fires in narrow back yards, pigpens, cowsheds, small two-story frame dwellings, barking dogs in the yard…all

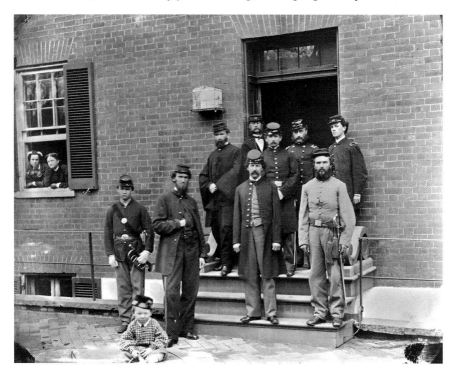

Civil War soldiers emerge from Miss Lydia English's Seminary for Young Women, a posh girls' school converted into a military hospital, near the end of the war in April 1865. *James Gardner. Courtesy Library of Congress.*

combined to endow this compact region of fifteen blocks with the air of a close village.[91]

The black refugees came to be known by the nickname "contrabands," based on an army general's assertion that escaped and abandoned slaves were "contraband of war." The contraband population officially recorded in the District of Columbia grew from four hundred in the spring of 1862 to forty-two hundred in the fall to seventeen thousand the following spring. By the time the war ended in April 1865, the number had spiraled to forty thousand.

Unlike slaves in the South, those living in Georgetown and other parts of the District of Columbia did not have to wait until the end of the Civil War to gain their freedom. On April 16, 1862, eight months before the Emancipation Proclamation, Congress passed the Compensated Emancipation Act, which freed slaves in the District and paid their owners an average of $300 each. Washington and Georgetown were the only cities in America to reimburse slave owners for the loss of their "property."[92]

When the war finally ended, the weary residents of Georgetown had barely begun converting the military barracks, hospitals and supply sheds back into homes, schools and churches when, on April 15, 1865, just five days after the Confederate surrender, the community was plunged into turmoil by the news of President Lincoln's assassination. Georgetown and Washington became the scene of a massive manhunt for assassin John Wilkes Booth and his accomplices.

One particularly unfortunate Georgetown resident that day was lawyer Joseph Henry Bradley, who was driving home in his buggy on a lonely road outside town when he was stopped and detained by police. When he protested that he had done nothing wrong, the agitated officers informed him that he was under arrest for the murder of the president of the United States. Bradley apparently bore such a striking resemblance to Booth that the police were convinced they had caught the killer. After some time, Bradley managed to get in touch with friends, who came to the jail and identified him. Apparently, lawmen had spent the day distributing "wanted posters" around town with Booth's likeness, and the picture looked remarkably like Bradley. The lawyer's wife told friends later that she "had thought that her colored servants had been behaving strangely all day" and speculated that they might have seen the poster, thought it was their employer and tipped the authorities.

But Bradley's association with the Lincoln shooting was not over. Some weeks after his mistaken arrest, Bradley served as counsel for John Surratt,

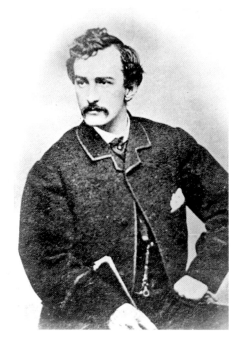

A photograph of Lincoln assassin John Wilkes Booth (1838–1865) taken by Alexander Gardner, photographer to the Army of the Potomac, in 1863. The picture was used on the "wanted poster" that was widely distributed by authorities looking for the president's killer. *Courtesy Library of Congress.*

one of the accused conspirators. Surratt admitted to scheming with Booth in an earlier plot to kidnap Lincoln and exchange him for Confederate prisoners. But when plans changed, Surratt dropped out of the conspiracy and was no longer involved when the abduction turned into a murder. With Bradley's legal assistance, Surratt was cleared, but his mother, Mary Surratt, was found guilty in a separate trial of being an accomplice in the assassination. She was hanged—the first woman ever to receive the death penalty in the United States. John Surratt managed to overcome the family stigma and became a teacher in the Washington area. He married a cousin of Francis Scott Key.[93]

Georgetown gradually returned to peacetime existence. Friends and relatives who had taken opposite sides in the war reconciled and rebuilt their lives. W.W. Corcoran came home from Europe and resumed his philanthropy, giving particular financial help to the battle-scarred South. Other Southern sympathizers like William Marbury went back to their old businesses and got used to life without the service of slaves.

But a few residents paid a high price for their roles as Rebels. A military officer named William Orton Williams and his cousin, Lieutenant W.G. Peter, were arrested as Confederate spies and hanged. The two were accused of infiltrating the Union ranks, using the phony names of "General W.C. Auton and Major Dunlop," to steal military secrets. Williams was a former aide to legendary Union general Winfield Scott, who served in the War of 1812 and the Mexican War and once ran for president. Williams also had been engaged to a daughter of Robert E. Lee, but the bride-to-be had died around the time the war began. Both young men were said to be related to original Georgetown mayor Robert Peter.[94]

WHO MOVED MY STREET?

Georgetown Joins Washington

After the Civil War, Georgetown's economy struggled. The latter decades of the 1800s were plagued by problems resulting from the surging population of refugees from the war-ravaged South and a decline in the tobacco and flour industries. A big reason for the drop-off in business was transportation. Since its beginnings as an Indian trading post, and through its heyday as an international export center, river transportation was the town's livelihood. If Georgetown was the heart of the region's trade with Europe and the Caribbean, then the Potomac was its main artery. But the artery was suffering frequent blockage.

Heavy spring and autumn rains brought floods and deposited enormous amounts of silt in the Potomac that could choke off navigation channels and halt shipping until the mud could be scooped away. The disruptions of river traffic year after year were bruising Georgetown's reputation as a dependable transportation hub. Most of the silt was runoff from vast acreage that had been converted from forest to farmland. Georgetown spent countless hours and millions of dollars in repair and dredging costs to keep the shipping lanes clear and facilities operating.

A particularly devastating flood hit the town in early October 1870, when churning waters wiped out several dock facilities and ruined sections of the Chesapeake and Ohio Canal. One account reported that the massive gates from several of the canal's locks could be seen floating away down the swollen Potomac. A massive logjam of silt and tangled trees obstructed navigation for weeks. An even worse flood came seven years later when heavy

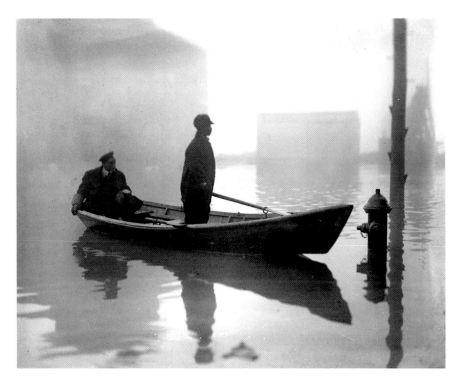

Spring and autumn rains brought frequent flooding to the Potomac, which deposited silt and debris that obstructed shipping lanes. High-water periods were so numerous in the early 1900s that some residents kept small boats to paddle through the flooded streets. *National Photo Company Collection (reproduction number 18676). Courtesy Library of Congress, Prints and Photographs Division.*

November rains unleashed a sudden wall of water that ripped apart docks and warehouses, filled cellars with mud, carved away several sections of the C&O Canal and left behind so much muck and debris that the Potomac was impassable again for weeks. These disruptions to commerce came on the heels of a winter freeze that iced over the river and canal system and also had shut down shipping.[95]

Bad weather wasn't the only problem. The new and more dependable railroad industry was taking away more shipping business from the waterways each day. As railroad and highway transportation eroded the Potomac's importance as a commercial shipping route, public attention shifted from clearing silt out of the river to building bridges over it.

One of the earliest structures to cross the Potomac at Georgetown, called the Aqueduct Bridge, was essentially an elevated waterway built to carry boats from the Chesapeake and Ohio Canal to the Alexandria Canal on the

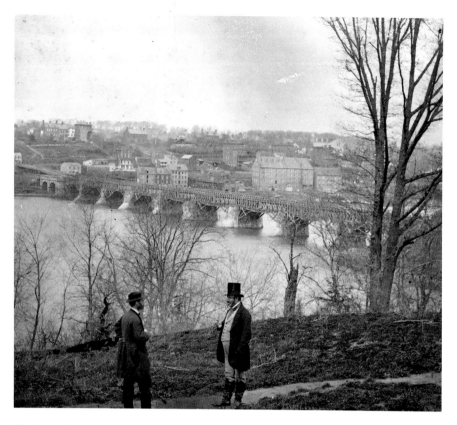

Gentlemen from the Civil War period meet on the Virginia side of the Aqueduct Bridge leading into Georgetown. *William Morris Smith. Courtesy Library of Congress.*

Virginia side of the river. But as the canal business waned, the bridge for boats was transformed into a road for horses, carriages and pedestrians. The bridges, like the wharves and canals, were subject to severe damage from frequent freshets—heavy seasonal floods that sent mud, tree limbs and other destructive debris churning down the river.

Georgetown's Potomac bridge was a long time coming. Talk of a span to Virginia dated back to the 1700s, but the owners and users of the wharfs always managed to kill the project. The shippers worried that bridges would create obstructions in the river that would worsen the problem of silt accumulation, hinder navigation and hurt their export business by preventing large ships from reaching the docks. The tobacco shippers, in particular, "regarded the bridge as injurious to the channel of the river, and a great detriment to the commerce of the town."

Historian Richard Plummer Jackson wrote that

> *the bridge is something Georgetown has always "thrown a brick at"* [and] *corporate authorities did their best to prevent the passage of the bill chartering the Potomac Bridge Company, which was incorporated February 5th, 1808.* [But] *what the town could not do, the Potomac River did for us. The freshet of 1829 broke the bridge asunder in many places, and the company, being unable to repair the same, sold all their right and title to the United States for twenty thousand dollars.*

Congress then appropriated money to rebuild the bridge.

Another iteration of a Potomac bridge, funded by congressional appropriations, "was thrown open for travel in the month of October 1835, when the President of the United States with his Cabinet crossed it on foot, and returned in carriages," Jackson wrote.

> *For some years the bridge escaped without any damage, but, in 1840, a portion of it was destroyed by an ice freshet. Without exact date, it is impossible to enumerate the different occasions in which it has been injured. It was injured by the freshets in 1856, 1860, 1863, and 1867; in several*

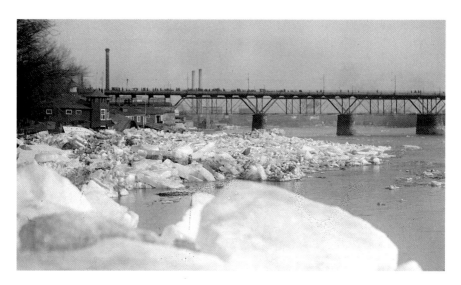

Winter freezes and spring rains often dislodged chunks of ice that flowed down the Potomac, inflicting damage on wharves and bridges. *National Photo Company Collection (reproduction number 28229). Courtesy Library of Congress, Prints and Photographs Division.*

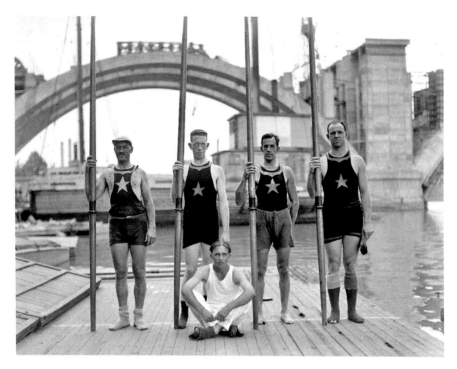

Rowing clubs were popular social endeavors in Georgetown. The Potomac Boat Club, founded in 1869, is among the oldest still operating. A crew gets ready to race, posing in front of an arch of the Key Bridge, under construction in 1921. *National Photo Company Collection, 1921 (reproduction number 04546). Courtesy Library of Congress, Prints & Photographs Division*

instances, spans of the bridge were carried away and travel suspended for several months at a time; but Congress has always been liberal in making appropriations to repair damage.[96]

The bridge was frequently out of service until the present arched concrete span was constructed between 1917 and 1923 and named in honor of Francis Scott Key, whose former house on M Street was torn down to make way for it. A small park honoring Key was built near the site. The new bridge was big, high and strong enough to withstand the ravages of the Potomac flooding, which persistently continued to cripple the canal system. In the 1870s, a group of Georgetown businessmen came up with an ingenious infrastructure project to bolster the efficiency of the waterways. Historian Richard Plummer Jackson noted,

A company was formed in 1875 to build and erect a railway or inclined plane, about a mile above Georgetown, that would pass loaded boats from the canal to the river without the trouble of passing through a series of locks.

The Potomac Lock and Dam Company's project would carry boats in a large water-filled "caisson" on railroad tracks.

Jackson described how the gigantic contraption worked:

A railway was constructed in a diagonal line to the river, some six hundred feet long, consisting of several tracks. On the middle track is the caisson, one hundred and twelve feet long, seventeen feet wide, and eight feet deep, closed at each end by gates. On each side of the caisson are several cars, filled with stone and rocks, to balance the caisson when descending the inclined plane with a loaded boat.[97]

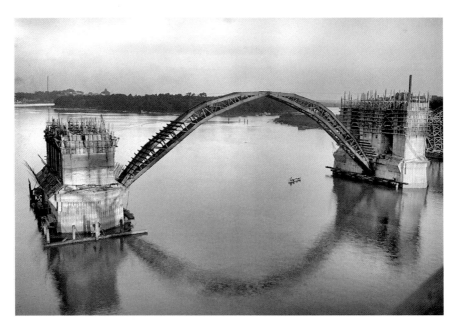

Construction of the Francis Scott Key Bridge, replacing the old Aqueduct Bridge, about 1920. The structure, built by the Army Corps of Engineers, was designed to withstand the floods and pressure from floating ice and other debris that had damaged and destroyed earlier spans. *National Photo Company Collection. Courtesy Library of Congress, Prints and Photographs Division.*

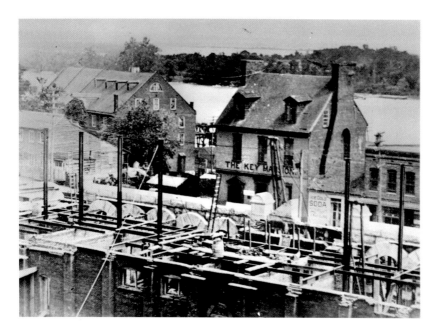

Construction in the 1890s near the Key Mansion, home of Francis Scott Key, at 3518 M Street. The house was opened to tourists sometime after Key's death in 1843. *HABS (reproduction number HABS DC, GEO 42-1). Courtesy Library of Congress, Prints and Photographs Division.*

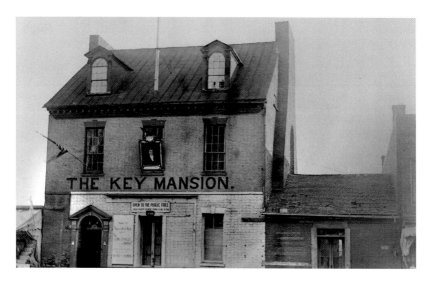

The home of national anthem author Francis Scott Key was one of Georgetown's top tourist attractions in the late 1800s. The house was torn down sometime before 1920 to make way for the new Francis Scott Key Bridge. *HABS (reproduction number HABS DC, GEO 42-2). Courtesy Library of Congress, Prints and Photographs Division.*

The innovative railroad for boats significantly cut travel time and allowed traffic to flow during times when the canal locks were closed for repairs, helping salvage some of the C&O's dwindling freight business.

While Georgetown grappled with postwar transportation challenges, the neighboring city of Washington was battling economic and infrastructure problems as well. The Civil War had left both towns in deplorable condition. Roads were unpaved—dust bins in dry weather and sloppy mudholes when it rained—and water supplies were inadequate for the swelling population. Sanitation also was a major concern, with some waterways becoming open sewers. In addition, such basic services as police and fire protection were often hindered by squabbling between the jurisdictions of Washington, Georgetown and unincorporated parts of the federal territory, also called Washington County. All three local governments were painfully short of cash. The City of Washington was so behind on its bills that creditors tried to repossess the furniture in the mayor's office. Meanwhile, the two dominant political parties—the antislavery Republican Party of the late Abraham Lincoln and the Democratic Party, which had been more sympathetic to the "states' rights" leanings of the South—were bitterly divided on most issues, impeding progress on sorely needed public improvements.

Things were so bad that some disgusted members of Congress proposed moving the capital elsewhere. Western lawmakers spearheaded a drive to abandon Washington for a new capital at St. Louis, prompting local politicians to drop their partisan disagreements and work together to keep the government from leaving town.

Leading the effort was Washington city councilman Alexander Shepherd, a Republican Party operative who was popular in the black community as an advocate of equal rights for former slaves. Shepherd convinced Congress to pass the Territory Act of 1871, which abolished the city charters of Washington and Georgetown and made the District of Columbia a single political entity with a unified territorial government. The new city-state, which included Georgetown, came to be called Washington, D.C.

Many former Georgetown officials took positions in the new regime. The first governor of the District was Georgetown financier Henry Cooke, who served a two-year term. Then, Shepherd won the post on a campaign of broad civic improvements, earning the nickname "Boss Shepherd" because of his forceful political talents. Shepherd immediately launched a barrage of projects to pave streets, build sidewalks, install new streetlights and water lines, consolidate police and fire departments, improve sanitation services, upgrade schools, establish parks and plant

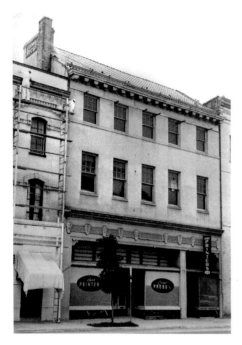

The City Tavern at 3206–08 M Street, built in 1796, had to convert its basement to the main floor when city improvement projects lowered the street level by about ten feet. The road project upset many residents of Georgetown, who had to build high staircases to reach their front doors, which were on street level prior to the "improvements." *Russell Jones, July 1959. Courtesy Library of Congress.*

trees. The work systematically transformed the newly expanded city of Washington from a grimy, overcrowded, mismanaged mess into a tightly run municipality. The District of Columbia was finally on its way to becoming the shining showplace of democracy that Washington, Jefferson and L'Enfant had envisioned a century earlier.

Shepherd's urban renewal program included filling in the Washington Canal, which had fallen into disuse and become a stinking sewer trench, paving 150 miles of roads, planting sixty thousand trees and installing 120 miles of wastewater culverts and storm drains, 39 miles of natural gas pipelines and 30 miles of water mains. In Georgetown, Shepherd's road and sewer projects changed the elevation of many streets, particularly near the waterfront. The elevation of Bridge Street, renamed M Street to conform to L'Enfant's original plan, was lowered between ten and sixteen feet in some places. The excavation turned the basements of several buildings into street-level floors and forced many homeowners to build high steps to their front doors, now suddenly located on the second floor. A number of the steep front-porch staircases can still be seen today. The current main floor of the historic City Tavern on M Street was originally the building's basement, but it became the front room when Boss Shepherd lowered the roadway.

Georgetown's citizens liked the new water and sewer services, but they hated the new street levels. The new District government had "uncontrollable power to dig down, fill up, and change the grade of the streets wherever they thought best," historian Jackson complained.

The Board of Public Works entered the town to make what they called improvements, in altering and changing the grade of the streets, to the great detriment and injury of a large class of property holders. If ever a set of sensible men were guilty of a wrong, it was in filling up Bridge Street between High and Market Streets.

A most serious injury was done to the property holders. The grade of the streets was destroyed, and all communication was cut off from the canal and river—the south side of the canal being twenty feet below the foot of Market Space. Your chronicler has seen thousands of hogsheads of tobacco, and barrels of flour, hauled to the river down Market Space, in days gone by, to the vessels at the wharves, to be shipped to Europe; but all this communication is now cut off, and stores and dwellings which formerly sold, before the grade of the street was destroyed, from three to four thousand dollars, would not bring at the present time more than one-third of that amount.[98]

The Shepherd government also built the city's first public transportation system, a network of streetcars that, despite some protests, allowed riders of all races. Residents found the transit system entertaining, as well as convenient. In Georgetown, "there were two lines of cars known as the upper and lower," local writer Josephine Davis Leary explained.

The one on Bridge Street (now M Street) was a cable car, while the other running on West Street (P Street) was a horse-drawn affair. If summer evenings dragged a bit in that period, the thoughtful head of a family often suggested a street-car ride to Lincoln Park on the upper line. The cars were open at that season and the trip, which allowed you to wave to friends on the sidewalk all along the route, consumed most of an evening and was considered a very pleasant diversion.

The cable cars, operated by an underground chain, required strong powers of balance on the part of the passengers for, as they entered at the rear and the cart started, they were jerked violently forward toward the boxed-in seat of the motorman, sometimes landing on that gentleman's shoulders. In winter, both lines of cars, lacking any heating arrangement, were insulated from the cold by thick layers of straw on the floor which at least prevented chilblains among the passengers. But it also led to the necessity for lady travelers, on alighting, to stand still a few minutes to pick, or have picked off, straws from the hems of their skirts before proceeding on their way.[99]

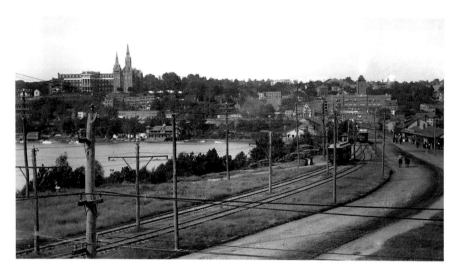

Early mass transit systems in Washington and Georgetown consisted of streetcars on railroad tracks. Some lines were cable cars and others were pulled by horses. *National Photo Company Collection, 1915 (reproduction number 20241). Courtesy Library of Congress, Prints and Photographs Division.*

The rapid transit system and all of Boss Shepherd's other improvements came with a high price. Typical of many government projects, the District of Columbia's face-lift overran its budget. When concerned members of Congress launched an audit, the District was found to be $13 million in arrears on its debt payments, and the nation's capital declared bankruptcy. Taxes soared to pay off the obligations, forcing some property owners to sell their homes when they could not afford the tax bills. As the debt piled up and tax rates escalated, Shepherd went from local hero to the target of investigations for political cronyism and mishandling public money. The "Boss" was fired, and the District's governor-led system was abolished and replaced with a Board of Commissioners appointed by the president and confirmed by the Senate.

Despite his financial and political problems, Shepherd's civic enhancements stopped any further talk of moving the federal government, and Georgetown adapted to being part of the capital city that it once served as the headquarters for building. But the community continued suffering from the decline of river commerce. The tobacco warehouses and shipping ports along the waterfront were gradually replaced by other industries. Many of the flour mills were retrofitted to process cotton and manufacture paper, cement, textiles, soap and other products. Former tobacco facilities were converted into pork processing plants and other sorts of smokestack factories that transformed the waterfront into a dirty, smelly industrial zone. The advent of electricity prompted the construction of one of the area's first power plants along the river in Georgetown.

Meanwhile, Georgetown's once elegant and sought-after neighborhoods deteriorated into one of Washington's worst slums. Around the turn of the century, it had become an area that most of polite society avoided. Lifelong resident Grace Dunlop Ecker illustrated the blight on the community's reputation with a story she heard from

> an old lady who has lived all her life in one of the loveliest old Georgetown houses. Many years ago, while the street cars were still drawn by horses, she was in a car sitting opposite two women, one of whom was pointing out the sights to the other. They passed Dupont Circle...and as they crossed the P Street Bridge, she said, "Now we are coming into Georgetown where nobody lives but colored people and a few white people who can't get away."[100]

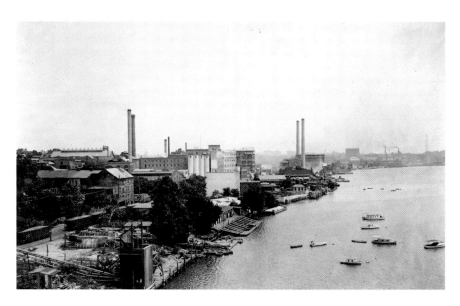

Around the turn of the century, the docks and warehouses along the Georgetown waterfront were converted to factories as manufacturing surpassed agriculture as an economic driver. *National Photo Company Collection (reproduction number 3C25564). Courtesy Library of Congress, Prints and Photographs Division.*

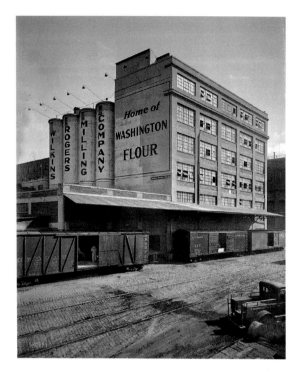

The Wilkins Rogers Milling Co. at 3261 K Street (formerly Water Street), one of the many flour mills that prospered in Georgetown between Civil War times and the mid-1900s. *National Photo Company Collection (reproduction number 33024). Courtesy Library of Congress, Prints & Photographs Division.*

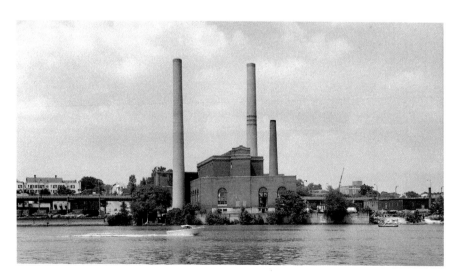

The Capital Traction Power Plant, built in 1911, at 3142 K Street. It was destroyed in 1968. *National Photo Company Collection, 1967. Courtesy Library of Congress.*

Ms. Ecker also recalled a 1916 conversation involving newly appointed Secretary of War Newton Baker, who had just arrived to serve in the administration of Woodrow Wilson.

> *At that time Georgetown had hardly begun to be fashionable again, and on first coming to Washington and hunting for a house, Mrs. Baker told a friend she was discouraged trying to find one with a yard where her three children could play, and that she thought they would have to go to Fort Myer. The friend answered in a tone of deep commiseration, "Too bad! You will have to pass through Georgetown!"*

Later, however, Mr. Baker moved to Georgetown anyway, occupying a house built in 1794 by Thomas Beall of George.

In addition to Secretary Baker, several residents and businesses stayed in Georgetown during the tough times and were instrumental in some of America's most important technological and scientific advancements during the late nineteenth and early twentieth centuries.

Famed inventor Alexander Graham Bell lived and worked in Georgetown at his Volta Laboratory and Bureau, which he founded to conduct research to aid the deaf and hard of hearing. Yet another Georgetowner who came to America from Scotland, Bell moved to the community in 1879 with his wife, who had been deaf since childhood. When the French government awarded Bell its Volta Prize of fifty thousand francs for inventing the telephone, he used the money to found a laboratory in Georgetown to study the recording and transmitting of sound. He then established the Volta Bureau to promote "the increase and diffusion of knowledge relating to the deaf." Originally headquartered at Bell's father's residence at 1527 Thirty-fifth Street, the Volta Bureau expanded into a new building that Bell constructed in 1893, a neoclassical yellow brick structure at 1537 Thirty-fifth Street, across the street from the family home.

Georgetown also can claim some credit for the advent of the computer age. In 1892, engineer and inventor Hermann Hollerith moved his newly established tabulating machine business from downtown Washington to an old building in Georgetown that once was a shop for making hogsheads, the big wooden barrels used for shipping tobacco. Hollerith, a former U.S. Census Bureau worker, designed a device to calculate and classify census data more efficiently. The Census Bureau had taken eight years to complete the 1880 population count and feared that the 1890 census would take even longer. Using an idea he developed while watching a train

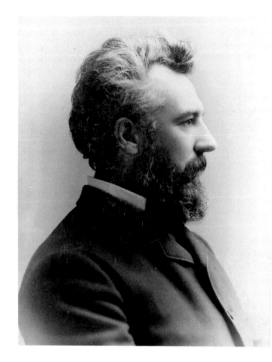

Left: Alexander Graham Bell (1847–1922), inventor of the telephone, lived and worked in Georgetown. *C.M. Bell, 1886. Courtesy Library of Congress, Gilbert H. Grosvenor Collection.*

Below: The Volta Bureau at 1537 Thirty-fifth Street, founded by Alexander Graham Bell to conduct research on sound and hearing loss. *HABS, original design as submitted by Peabody & Stearns (reproduction number HABS DC, GEO, 115-7). Courtesy Library of Congress, Prints and Photographs Division.*

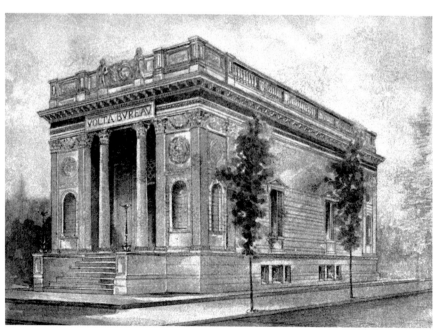

conductor punch tickets, Hollerith invented a machine that used electrical signals to "read" holes in paper or cards that passed over metal contacts. Hollerith made his punch cards the same size as dollar bills, which allowed him to save manufacturing costs by incorporating common money-storage bins into the devices.

He sold his prototype instrument to the U.S. Army for compiling medical statistics and then won a contract to make machines for the 1890 population count. By automating the census, the newfangled appliances accomplished in one year what would have taken ten years of hand tabulating, saving the government $5 million. It was the beginning of modern data processing. In 1896, Hollerith incorporated the Tabulating Machine Company to build and distribute his invention, which made him a millionaire. In 1911, the company merged with other firms to become the Computing-Tabulating-Recording Company, later called the International Business Machines Corporation, which became computer giant IBM.

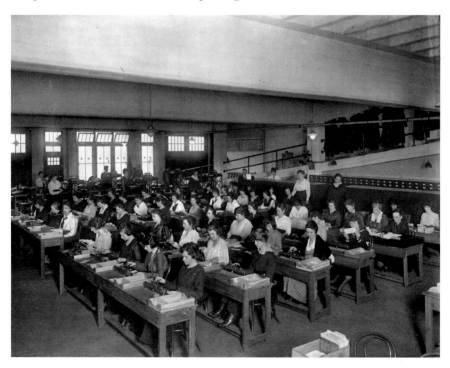

Workers at Hermann Hollerith's Tabulating Machine Company, housed in a building that was once used to make tobacco hogsheads. The company, which developed the machines to automate the census count, grew over the years to become computer giant IBM Corporation. *Photograph by Harris & Ewing (reproduction number 20580). Courtesy Library of Congress, Prints and Photographs Division.*

Another American pioneer of science, Dr. Walter Reed, also lived in Georgetown during the 1890s and early 1900s. A physician in the U.S. Army Medical Corps, Reed spent years working at military posts in the western territories, tending to the healthcare needs of U.S. soldiers and, occasionally, to Indians, including the famous Apache chief Geronimo. An expert in investigating the causes of disease, Reed moved to Georgetown in 1893 to join the new Army Medical School, where he was a professor of bacteriology and clinical microscopy. As part of his research, Reed traveled to Cuba in 1899 and 1900 to study tropical ailments that were afflicting U.S. troops, including yellow fever, whose fearsome epidemics had claimed hundreds of thousands of American lives since early colonial times. Reed's team determined that yellow fever was spread by mosquito bites and not, as widely believed, by clothing and bedding that had come into contact with sick patients or their bodily fluids.

Using volunteers as human subjects for experiments, Reed and fellow physician Carlos Finlay discovered the microbe that caused yellow fever and worked on ways to control it. The army credits Reed and Finlay with significantly lowering the mortality rates among workers building the Panama Canal and other projects in mosquito-infested tropical zones.

Ms. Ecker, who grew up in the famous doctor's neighborhood, wrote about her frequent childhood visits to his Q Street home:

> *I recall a most delightful party at the Reeds' on St. Valentine night in 1899, given for friends of their son. When the invitations were sent out, we were told the name of the young man or girl to whom our valentine was to be written. It was at the time of the tremendous blizzard of that year, and we walked to the party between drifts of snow piled higher than our heads. But it was anything but cold when we got inside—open fires and jollity! Dr. Reed read aloud the poems, one by one, and we had to guess the authors and to whom they were addressed. In the library, ensconced in mysterious gloom, seated in a corner on the floor was a fortune-teller. It was a perfect party!*[101]

Georgetown continued gaining new factories and losing affluent residents. Many moved to new mansions that were being built across Rock Creek along Washington's Massachusetts Avenue, while others established country estates just outside of town. One wooded tract on the northwest edge of Georgetown was owned by longtime resident Thomas Hume, a friend of former president Ulysses Grant, who also once lived in Georgetown. A local legend says that one day Grant was visiting Hume at the country property, which contained a large walnut orchard, and the two men were discussing potential names for the place. Hume wanted to call it something like "Walnut Grove," but another nearby property already had a walnut-related title. So Grant suggested, "Why not turn walnut around and call it Tunlaw?" Hume loved the idea, and for years he delighted in telling people that President Grant had come up with the idea of spelling walnut backward. The street passing through the area, running a few blocks west of Wisconsin Avenue, is still named Tunlaw.[102]

Georgetown finally began to recover from its sad period of neglect and disrepute during the 1930s. President Franklin Roosevelt's New Deal greatly expanded the size and scope of government, and waves of bureaucrats began streaming into Washington to fill federal jobs created by the new programs. With housing suddenly at a premium all across the District, several of Roosevelt's top officials found homes in Georgetown, setting off a new era of rebuilding and gentrification. The Great Depression made Georgetown popular again. One historic residence that became a center of activity during the Roosevelt years was the "Big Red House on R Street," at number 3238. The old residence had been owned by General H.W. Halleck, army chief of staff during the Civil War. After the war, Grant lived there until he became president. In the early days of the New Deal, the place was rented by a group of young administration officials, led by Tommy Corcoran and Benjamin Cohen, known as the "Hot Dog Boys," who drafted and promoted passage of landmark legislation. The bills included the Securities and Exchange Act, the Fair Labor Standards Act and the Public Utility Holding Company Act of 1935, which regulated the size and financial operations of the nation's electric power companies. The house was a round-the-clock center of activity for administration officials collaborating on policy and legislation.[103]

One of the key events in Georgetown during the Roosevelt years was the Dumbarton Oaks Conference, which led to the formation of the United Nations. The historic meeting took place from August 21 to October 7, 1944, at Dumbarton Oaks, a sprawling estate built on the Heights of Georgetown by early tobacco barons. The conference brought together representatives of four major global powers—Great Britain, the United States, China and the Soviet Union—at the height of World War II. U.S. secretary of state Cordell Hull opened the session, declaring that "peace, like liberty, requires constant devotion and ceaseless vigilance" and calling on the four "united nations" to "create the international foundations for a just and lasting peace."

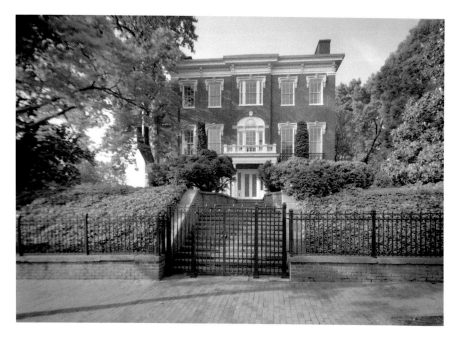

The "Big Red House" at 3238 R Street, also known as the Scott-Grant House, former home of President Ulysses Grant, Civil War army chief of staff H.W. Halleck and Roosevelt administration officials Tommy Corcoran and Ben Cohen, who drafted several important pieces of New Deal legislation. *HABS (reproduction number HABS DC, GEO, 242-1). Courtesy Library of Congress, Prints and Photographs Division.*

The delegations were led by Hull; U.S. undersecretary of state Edward Reilly Stettinius; British permanent undersecretary of state for foreign affairs Sir Alexander Cadogan; ambassador to the United States and Earl of Halifax Edward Wood; Soviet ambassador to the United States Andrei Gromyko; and Chinese ambassador to the United Kingdom Wellington Koo.

The conference, officially known as "Washington Conversations on International Organization, Dumbarton Oaks," chose the name of the participating countries' wartime alliance, the United Nations (UN), for the new world body. Patterned after the earlier League of Nations championed by President Woodrow Wilson following World War I, the new UN would include a Security Council, a General Assembly, a Secretariat and an International Court of Justice. But the conferees modified several rules and procedures that had hampered the effectiveness of the League of Nations and led to its demise.

The Dumbarton Oaks Conference further elevated Georgetown's renewed status as an important and sophisticated part of Washington.

In the years following World War II, more business leaders, politicians and diplomats began moving back to Georgetown and restoring its classic old homes. Prominent newcomers included Dean Acheson, who served as secretary of state under President Harry Truman, and Massachusetts senator John F. Kennedy and his wife, Jackie, who were leading fixtures of Georgetown social life until their move to the White House after the election of 1960. The glamour of the Kennedy administration proved to be another enormous boost to the social revival of Georgetown, and Mrs. Kennedy moved back to the neighborhood following her husband's assassination in 1963. Other high-visibility Georgetown residents included *Washington Post* publishers Philip and Katherine Graham, whose R Street mansion was the scene of numerous high-society events through the years, including dinner parties regularly attended by presidents, congressional leaders and high-ranking diplomats.

Joining Dumbarton Oaks and other old mansions on the Heights of Georgetown, where so much history was made, stands another stately building where much of that history has been preserved. The classic old Georgetown Branch of the District of Columbia Public Library, at the intersection of Wisconsin Avenue and R Street, for many years housed the locally famous Peabody Room, named for philanthropist George Peabody, who funded the first public library in the city. The second-floor Peabody Room held a priceless collection of documents, paintings, photographs and other material chronicling Georgetown's history back to the days of the Indian village of Tohoga in the early 1600s.

The Peabody Room gave Georgetown a historical repository unique among American communities. But in late April 2007, fire swept through the old brick library, with its irreplaceable trove of Georgetown memorabilia that scholars had been collecting for 140 years. Many items were destroyed or damaged by smoke and water. More than four hundred boxes of archival materials were recovered from the smoldering building and sent to conservation facilities. Two years were required for the Peabody Room's special collections librarian Jerry McCoy to reprocess the materials and to organize them for access by the public. True to the history of the local government, money was in short supply for restoring the damaged artwork, photographs and books and repairing their burned-out home. Reprocessing of the Peabody Room materials was carried out at the D.C. Public Library's Washingtoniana Division, located in the Martin Luther King Jr. Memorial Library in downtown Washington, while work progressed to rebuild the historic Georgetown branch.

PREACHING, TEACHING AND PULLING TEETH

Churches and Schools

Education and religion have always been central to life in Georgetown. The colony of Maryland was founded as an enclave for Roman Catholics to freely practice their faith, and Catholics were instrumental in establishing the region's early social and civic institutions. Another major religious force in Georgetown was the Presbyterian Church, the traditional denomination of the many settlers from Scotland.

The earliest Roman Catholic congregation in Georgetown was the Trinity Church, with records of marriages and baptisms going back to April 1795. Its first pastor was the Reverend Francis Neale, who had arrived by 1792. Founded by Jesuits, Trinity is the oldest continuously operating church in the District of Columbia. The congregation met in several buildings before constructing its present sanctuary on N Street. Its earlier chapels were used by Georgetown College, also founded by Jesuits, for commencements and other ceremonies during the early days of the school.

Georgetown's Presbyterian congregation, by far the dominant religious institution for much of the town's history, was led for half a century by the Reverend Stephen Bloomer Balch, a colorful, high-profile and much-beloved leader who preached a famous memorial service for his friend George Washington in 1799. Balch, born in Maryland in 1746, was a graduate of Princeton, where he studied under clergyman and Declaration of Independence signer John Witherspoon. A firm believer in education, as well as religion, Balch always operated schools in conjunction with his churches. He came to Georgetown in 1780 and preached his first sermon in a little log building somewhere along present-day Wisconsin Avenue.

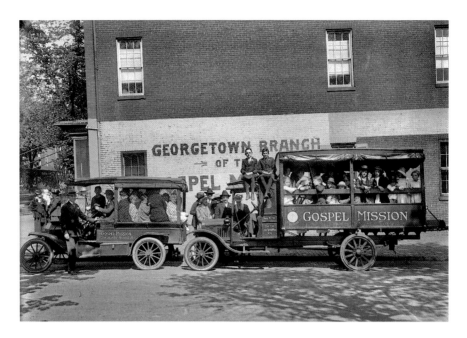

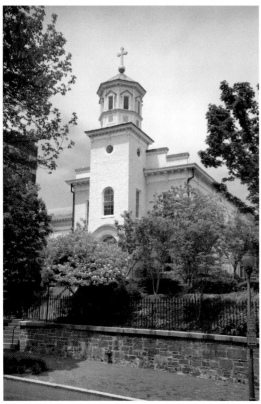

Above: Religion has always been a fixture of Georgetown, including colonial-era churches and, in the early twentieth century, traveling evangelists. *National Photo Company Collection (reproduction number 29082). Courtesy Library of Congress, Prints and Photographs Division.*

Left: Trinity Church, the first Roman Catholic congregation in Georgetown, at 3513 N Street. *Photo by Missy Loewe.*

Balch's engaging personality and dynamic oratorical skills helped build a tremendous following. George Washington came from Mount Vernon, more than fifteen miles away, to worship, and Thomas Jefferson also attended Balch's services. Many of the town's founding Scottish settlers belonged to the congregation, whose official "pew holders" included Thomas Beall of George. In addition to Balch's popularity, another reason for the church's heavy attendance was its status as "the only Protestant house of worship for miles around at that time."

A history of the congregation boasts that during Balch's early tenure, the Georgetown Presbyterian Church

> was "the" church of the District this side of the Potomac; all denominations attended here. Methodists, Episcopalians and others, as well as the Presbyterians, received the word of God at the mouth of the Presbyterian pastor, and communed together at the same altar. Such was the liberality that prevailed in those days.[104]

By 1806, the church had outgrown its original home and built a larger sanctuary and graveyard a few blocks away. Because "the lot adjoining the old church was used as a burying ground," resident Sally Somervell Mackall remembered, "these bodies were dug up, many of them put in boxes and packed in the chapel cellar of the Presbyterian cemetery, where they were knocked about in every direction, the boys in the neighborhood enjoying playing foot-ball with some of the skulls." Horror-stricken church elders promptly recovered the desecrated craniums, disciplined the errant athletes and made sure the skeletons were properly reinterred.[105]

Most towns in colonial America had strong Episcopal congregations, reflecting the official Anglican faith of settlers from England. The first Anglican church in Georgetown was the St. John's Episcopal parish, formed in the 1790s. The Reverend C.M. Butler, St. John's rector in the 1840s, wrote that

> the first movement toward establishing an Episcopal Church in this place was made by the Reverend Mr. Addison, with the concurrence and assistance of the Reverend Dr. Balch, a Presbyterian clergyman, whose memory is still warmly cherished in this community.
>
> Hearing that there were some Episcopal families in this place, [Addison] paid it a visit; was invited by Dr. Balch to hold an Episcopal service in his church, and encouraged by him to endeavor to organize an Episcopal

congregation. This incident is in perfect accordance with the character which this venerated man left behind him for Christian kindness and liberality. Mr. Addison continued to visit the place and to hold services occasionally during the years 1794 and 1795. In the summer of 1796, the first effort, of which any record remains, was made to organize a congregation and build a church.

Georgetown's Episcopals organized membership committees and began raising funds for a building, but the new sanctuary "was carried up only to the first range of windows" when the congregation ran out of money and construction stopped. "During this period the Reverend Mr. Addison held occasional services in this place, though with little encouragement to his hopes of completing the building," Butler reported, adding that a subsequent funding drive, kicked off at a Friday night meeting in 1803 at "Mr. Semmes' tavern," helped garner 154 "subscribers," among whom were Thomas Jefferson and Reverend Balch.[106]

To commemorate the community's history, a large boulder in the St. John's churchyard displays a plaque honoring Ninian Beall, considered by many to be the "father of Georgetown." The inscription reads:

COLONEL NINIAN BEALL, born Scotland 1625, died Maryland 1717, patentee of Rock of Dumbarton, member of the House of Burgesses, Commander in Chief of Provincial Forces of Maryland. In grateful recognition of his services "upon all incursions and disturbances of neighboring Indians," the Maryland Assembly of 1699 passed "an act of gratuity." This memorial erected by the Society of Colonial Wars in the District of Columbia, 1910.

By 1817, Georgetown's original Episcopal church had grown sufficiently that a second parish was established, called Christ Church. Its organizational meeting was held in the home of former mayor Thomas Corcoran, who founded the new church along with Francis Scott Key. Additional Episcopal parishes were established as well, including Grace Church, built near the waterfront in the 1840s to minister to seamen and families of workers on the wharves and the C&O Canal.[107]

Other early congregations included a Methodist group that struggled financially, meeting in schools and the sanctuaries of other churches until it could afford its own building. When the Methodists finally purchased a lot in 1829, legal entanglements arose, and the property was confiscated

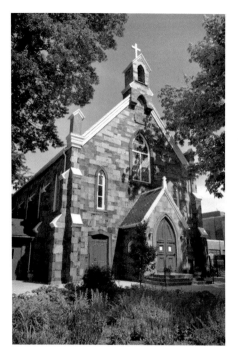

Grace Episcopal Church, established near the waterfront at 1041 Wisconsin Avenue in the 1840s to serve the religious needs of sailors, dockhands, C&O canal workers and others living and working near the river. *Photo by Missy Loewe.*

to pay the previous owner's back taxes. But philanthropist W.W. Corcoran bought the property out of receivership and handed it over to the church as a gift.[108]

The first Protestants to own land in Georgetown, but apparently with little religious activity to show for it, were the Lutherans. Colonel Charles Beatty, one of the town's original settlers, set aside a lot in 1769 for the use of the Lutheran Church. The local Lutheran community was a small group of German immigrants who built a schoolhouse on the land and began using its grounds as a cemetery. But no one seems to recall any regular worship services being held there.

Lutheran clergyman John J. Suman lamented in the late 1800s that "the condition of the Lutheran Church for the past half century has been rather deplorable" in Georgetown.

In the memory of the oldest inhabitant (Mr. Hurdle), there has not been any regular preaching of the gospel...until very recently. The lot on which the present building is erected was for a long time unenclosed, and the resting places of the sacred dead were trampled upon by the unhallowed feet of man and beast.

He added that

from various causes, the school was not a very great success— mismanagement, improper qualifications in some of the teachers, and want of proper support, operated to bring the school into disrepute and prevent its being of any advantage to the church.

But the congregation resolved its problems, upgraded the facilities and in 1870 a newly renovated church building "was re-dedicated to the worship of Almighty God," Suman reported. "It was a great day for us few Lutherans."[109]

Several of Georgetown's early churches welcomed all races, although many kept black members segregated in rear sections or balconies and required separate "colored" entrances. A few exclusively African American congregations formed, including the Mt. Zion Methodist Episcopal Church, along with the "Colored Baptist Church" and the Ebenezer Church, founded with 150 members in 1856. The Ebenezer congregation also operated a school with 160 students, 2 superintendents and 17 teachers.[110]

Mt. Zion Methodist Episcopal, known today as Mt. Zion United Methodist Church at 1334 Twenty-ninth Street, began around 1814 when black members left the mostly white Montgomery Street Church. Because black children had limited access to public schools at the time, the Mt. Zion Church also became an educational center for blacks in the community, teaching adults as well as children. During the Civil War period, a temporary burial vault in Mt. Zion's cemetery served as a hideout for the Underground Railroad, sheltering runaway slaves who were fleeing north.

In addition to its historic churches, Georgetown also boasts one of America's oldest institutions of higher learning. Georgetown College was founded by clergyman John Carroll in January 1789 to provide a Roman Catholic education for young men in Maryland. Carroll, who later became the first archbishop of Baltimore, located his college atop a high hill on the community's western border. Carroll had begun raising funds a few years earlier for his "academy, at George-town, Patowmack-River, Maryland," telling potential donors, "On this academy are built all of my hopes of permanency and success of our holy religion in the United States." The first student, William Gaston of North Carolina, enrolled in the fall of 1791. He went on to become a member of Congress and a justice of his home state's Supreme Court.

An early set of instructions to parents advised that

> on entering the College, every pupil shall pay ten dollars. He shall bring a mattress, a pillow, two pillow cases, two pairs of sheets, four blankets and a counterpane, or pay $6.00 per annum for the use of bed and bedding. He must also bring with him one suit of clothes, as a uniform—which is in winter a blue cloth coat and pantaloons with a black velvet waistcoat; in summer white pantaloons with a black silk waistcoat are used. He must

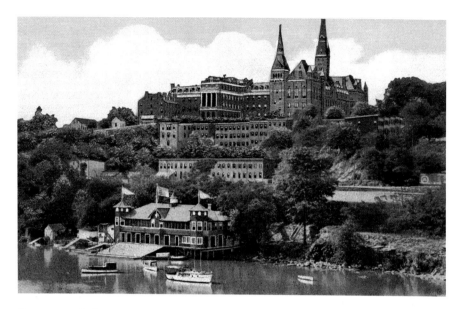

Georgetown College towers above the waterfront in a postcard picture from the early 1900s.

likewise bring with him two suits for daily wear, for which no particular color is prescribed; six shirts, six pairs of stockings, six pocket handkerchiefs, three pairs of shoes, a hat and a cloak or great coat, also a silver spoon. These articles if not brought by the student will be furnished by the College and included in the first bill.

The admissions department also noted that

the pension for board, washing, mending and mending materials, use of books (philosophical and mathematical excepted), pens, ink, and writing paper, slates and pencil, is $150. Medical aid and medicine, unless parents choose to run the risk of a doctor's bill in case of sickness, $3.00 per annum. All charges must be paid half-yearly in advance. With regard to pocket money it is desired that all students should be placed on an equality and that it should not exceed 12½ cents per week; and whatever is allowed must be deposited in the hands of the directors of the College.[111]

The new institution built a solid reputation for academic excellence, punctuated by President George Washington's visit to the campus in 1797, when he addressed the student body from the front porch of the Old North

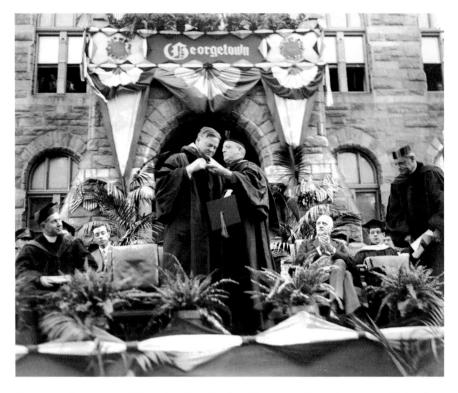

Commerce Secretary and future President Herbert Hoover speaks at Georgetown University on June 8, 1926. The school has a long tradition of visits by presidents and other national leaders. George Washington spoke there in 1797. President Lincoln addressed students before the Civil War. Many other chief executives have appeared there as well, including Georgetown alumnus Bill Clinton. *National Photo Company Collection (reproduction number 15932). Courtesy Library of Congress, Prints and Photographs Division.*

Building. The speech established a long tradition of presidents visiting the school. The college attained university status in 1815. In 1830, construction of an infirmary brought the first hospital beds to Georgetown, which led to the formation some years later, in 1850, of the Georgetown Medical School. In 1844, the school built one of the nation's earliest astronomical observatories, which was used to officially determine the latitude and longitude of Washington. The university also developed a highly regarded law school; drama and debating societies that are among the oldest in the United States; and championship rowing clubs, whose sleek, slender racing boats regularly ply the Potomac. Georgetown University was a mostly male institution, except for its school of nursing, until it went coed in the 1960s. In later years, Georgetown also was known for its nationally ranked basketball team.

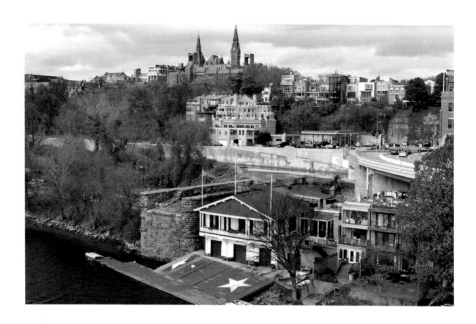

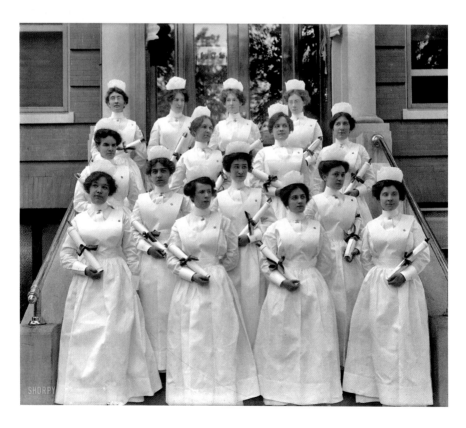

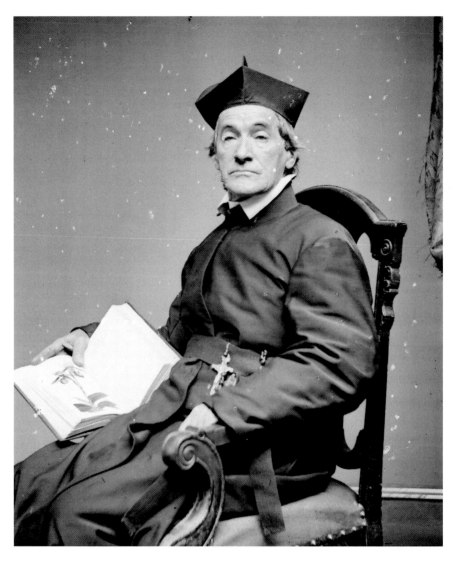

Roman Catholic Cardinal James Curley (1796–1889), one of Georgetown University's most revered faculty members, was the first director of the school's astronomical observatory during his sixty-year career at the institution. *Brady-Handy Collection (reproduction number 03535). Courtesy Library of Congress, Prints and Photographs Division.*

Opposite, top: The headquarters of the Potomac Boat Club at 3530 Water Street. The towers of Georgetown University loom in the background. *Photo by Missy Loewe.*

Opposite, bottom: Nursing students were among the first women admitted to Georgetown University, founded in the late 1700s as a male-only institution. This is the nursing school's graduating class from 1910. *Photograph by Harris & Ewing (reproduction number 20533). Courtesy Library of Congress, Prints and Photographs Division.*

The onset of the Civil War was a difficult time for Georgetown University. In 1859, the debating society took on the subject of secession, and when Rebel sympathizers won the contest, a brawl ensued and debates were canceled for the next year. Fistfights frequently broke out between Northern and Southern students. When the war began, 925 scholars dropped out to join the Confederate army, and 216 signed up to fight for the Union, while the federal government commandeered campus buildings for military use.

After the war, Georgetown's reputation was tarnished by associations with the Lincoln assassination. Actor and assassin John Wilkes Booth was known to associate with the school's drama society, and drama student David Herold accompanied Booth on his escape. He was convicted in the plot and hanged. Georgetown alumnus Samuel Mudd, also charged in the conspiracy, was the physician who set Booth's broken leg, suffered when he famously leaped onto the stage at Ford's Theatre after gunning down the president. But the university soon recovered its reputation as "the alma mater of hundreds of distinguished and meritorious citizens of the Republic…men who have carried with them to their distant and nearer homes…the training of high scholarship and the promptings of an honorable ambition," as proclaimed by a graduate in 1871.[112]

Not far from the Georgetown University campus is another historic Roman Catholic institution, one of the oldest convents in America, where, according to historian Jackson, "ladies live in single blessedness." About the year 1792, nuns fleeing the French Revolution sought refuge in Maryland and "endeavored to support themselves by opening a school, but they had to struggle constantly with poverty."[113]

Ms. Ecker noted that "these women, barefooted, according to the rule of their order, came of noble blood and had been born to luxury," but "once, it is told, they were reduced to such poverty that they had to sell a parrot, which they had as a pet, in order to save themselves from starvation." The "pious ladies of the monastery," as they were known around town, slowly increased their numbers, and in 1816, the Georgetown Visitation Convent established the first formal U.S. presence for the Order of the Visitation of Holy Mary. The order was founded in France in 1610 "to give to God daughters of prayer, and souls so interior, that they may be found worthy to serve His infinite majesty and to adore Him in spirit and in truth."[114]

Jackson, in his 1878 book *The Chronicles of Georgetown, D.C.*, recalled attending a chapel service for new nuns joining the order:

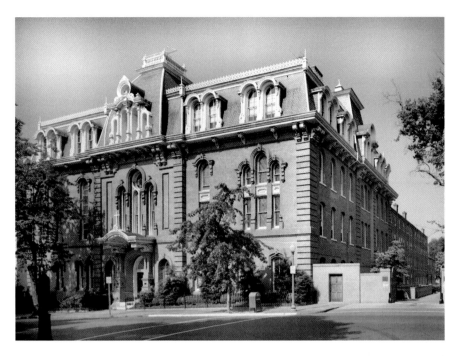

Georgetown Visitation Convent, at 1500 Thirtieth Street, the official first U.S. presence for the Sisters of the Visitation, a Roman Catholic religious order founded in 1610 in France. *HABS (reproduction number HABS GEO, 147-1). Courtesy Library of Congress, Prints and Photographs Division.*

The chronicler had the pleasure, many years past, to witness at the monastery the "taking of the veil" by four young ladies (whose names he will not mention, as it might be a breach of politeness to place the names of ladies in print without their consent).

The ladies who were the all-absorbing interest of the ceremony were young, beautiful, and tastefully arrayed in white. The Archbishop, in his canonicals, advanced to the front of the altar, and eloquently addressed the congregation and the novices who were about to enter as members of the Sisters of the Visitation. When the discourse was finished, the Archbishop gave a blessing, after which the novices one by one answered the questions which prepared them to renounce the world. Then coming forward for the last time, their baptismal names were renounced and they received their new titles. Thus they passed away from the gaze of their relatives and friends, and the sight of the world, of which their beauty and accomplishments would have rendered them the admiration and the ornament...They abandoned the cares and vexations of this life, of which they were too young to have felt any of its vicissitudes, to look forward to another world beyond the grave.[115]

In addition to the institutions for religious education, other private academies and public schools made an imprint on Georgetown.

When philanthropist Edward Magruder Linthicum died in 1869, he bequeathed money for a new school, but the endowment met with controversy among advocates of racial equality. In his will, Linthicum said:

Convinced that knowledge and piety constitute the only assurance of happiness and healthful progress to the human race…I give…the sum of fifty thousand dollars in trust, to found, establish, and maintain, in Georgetown…a free school for the education and instruction of indigent white boys and youths of said Georgetown in useful learning, and in the spirit and practice of Christian virtue.[116]

Because Georgetown was part of a federal territory, incorporating a new and much-needed public school required action by Congress. But several lawmakers, led by Massachusetts senator Charles Sumner, were outraged by the segregationist strings attached to Linthicum's legacy of "Christian virtue." Eventually, differences were settled, and the Linthicum Institute opened in 1872. As part of the deal, the school building also would house the Peabody Public Library, fulfilling the wishes of another wealthy Georgetown benefactor, financier George Peabody.[117]

In 1875, the Linthicum Institute added Georgetown's first night school to accommodate

a class of boys and youths of more advanced years…whose necessities require them to spend the day in work rather than in school…and after the daily toil is ended, they may resort for such practical instructions as will qualify them for the active duties and business of life.

The night school offered courses in "penmanship, book-keeping, drawing, arithmetic, geometry, chemistry and physics, the two last being taught experimentally."[118]

In 1811, a group of ninety-five residents established the Georgetown Lancaster School, with male and female "sides," to supplement the public school system's shortage of classroom space for girls. It was the second Lancaster School in America—the first was started five years earlier in New

York—modeled after Quaker academies in England run by pioneering educator George Lancaster, who incorporated the novel approach of having students help instruct one another.[119]

In the public school system, money was always tight, with parents and civic benefactors supplementing the often meager appropriations from Congress, which directed the school board to distribute funds "without discrimination as to color" of the students. There was, however, discrimination in the payroll department, with complaints that female instructors were paid only half as much as their male counterparts.[120]

In addition to their academic responsibilities, Georgetown's schoolteachers in the 1800s sometimes were called upon for dental duty. Historians report that

> *in September 1853 the board ordered that Mr. Craig, the principal teacher of the male school, be allowed five dollars to purchase instruments for pulling teeth. The extraction of teeth was not a punishment, but the toothache was such a common excuse for neglect of lessons and for non-attendance at school, that Mr. Craig came to the conclusion that the removal of the offending member was the best way of maintaining discipline. And it was astonishing...to see the business he did! Odontaglia became so contagious or fashionable that Mr. Craig soon filled a quart-cup, more or less, with trophies of his dentistry.[121]*

GHOST TOWN

Historic Houses and Noteworthy Neighbors

The march of progress and the ravages of time have eliminated far too many of the historic old homes in Georgetown. But a good number of interesting and noteworthy houses still grace the narrow streets, and a few remain in the hands of the families who built them in the eighteenth and early nineteenth centuries.

One of the earliest and most interesting mansions on the Heights of Georgetown is Dumbarton House, dating back to the Adams and Jefferson administrations. Called one of the very finest and most beautiful houses in the United States, the stately brick residence was built on part of Ninian Beall's original Rock of Dumbarton estate. Its owners have included Revolutionary War general Uriah Forrest and Gabriel Duval, the U.S. comptroller of the currency who later became a Supreme Court justice.

Joseph Nourse, also a veteran of the Revolutionary War and registrar of the U.S. Treasury under the first six presidents, bought the house in 1805 and lived there until 1813. Nourse supervised the monumental task of moving the Treasury Department's records from Philadelphia to the new capital in Washington in the early 1800s. He entertained a number of high-ranking guests in the house, including Thomas Jefferson, James Madison, James Monroe and John Quincy Adams. Nourse sold the house to Charles Carroll, who renamed it Bellevue. Carroll brought First Lady Dolley Madison to the house when she fled the Burning of Washington during the War of 1812.

The mansion changed hands several times through the years, and in 1915, it was declared an impediment to progress when the District of Columbia

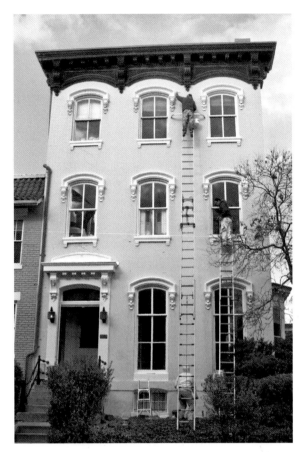

Left: As Georgetown regained popularity, people began buying and fixing up older houses, and residential prices rose in a long period of gentrification. *Photo by Missy Loewe.*

Below: Dumbarton House, at 2715 Q Street, dating from the Adams and Jefferson administrations. It was here where Dolley Madison took refuge when the British burned the White House in 1814. Headquarters of the National Society of the Colonial Dames of America, the house was moved several yards in 1915 to make room for a new road. *HABS (reproduction number HABS DC, GEO, 09-5). Courtesy Library of Congress, Prints and Photographs Division.*

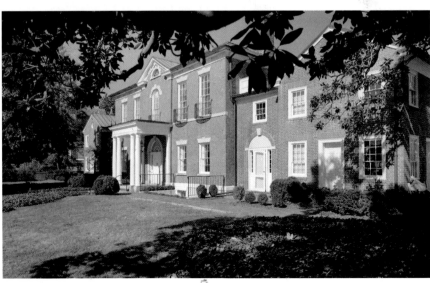

government built the "Buffalo Bridge," an ornate structure decorated by life-size statues of bison at each entrance. The bridge was to be a new connection between Georgetown and downtown Washington. To accommodate the increased traffic, the city planned to straighten the crooked Q Street. Bellevue, because it stood in the way, was slated for demolition. But loud protests from history-conscious neighbors prompted an official change of heart, and the city decided to move Bellevue rather than tear it down. Experts were hired to devise a way to shift the mansion several yards from its original position. The house moving was a big event in Georgetown, and scores of curious neighbors showed up to witness the engineering spectacle.

One of the onlookers was historian Grace Dunlop Ecker, who recalled:

> *Slowly, very, very slowly, old Bellevue was placed on huge rollers, horses were attached to a windlass, and it almost took a microscope to see the progress made day by day, but at last it reached its present site, safe and sound.*

The building's name was later changed to Dumbarton House, and in 1928, it was purchased by the National Society of the Colonial Dames of America for its national headquarters. The historic preservation group now operates the house as a museum.[122]

Another famous home on the Heights of Georgetown is Tudor Place. The regal yellow-colored stone structure was begun by tobacco magnate Francis Lowndes in 1794 on land purchased from Thomas Beall of George. Lowndes sold the unfinished home in 1805 to Thomas Peter, the son of Georgetown's first mayor. The Peters used their inheritance from Mrs. Peter's grandmother, Martha Washington, to finish the house under the supervision of U.S. Capitol architect William Thornton.

The Peters had eight children while living at Tudor Place, including daughters named America, Columbia and Britannia. Tudor Place remained in the Peter family until the 1980s, when it became a museum. The house contained the Peters' collection of Washington family memorabilia, including Martha Washington's seed-pearl wedding jewelry and dress, a set of china made for and presented to General Washington by the French government and a small camp trunk the first president used in his travels.

The Peters' youngest daughter, Britannia, was a bridesmaid in the wedding of her cousin Mary Custis (both girls were great-granddaughters of Martha Washington) when she married future Confederate commander Robert E. Lee. The Lees lived across the Potomac from Georgetown in a columned hilltop home called Arlington House, which was visible from Tudor Place.

Ms. Ecker related a "delicious story" she heard from a friend of Mary Custis about how the children of the Lee and Peter families communicated across the Potomac:

> *There being no telephones, when the girls at Arlington and at Tudor Place wanted to get together they had a series of signals. Hanging a red flannel petticoat out of the window meant "come on over." A white one had another meaning. This method was not popular with the owners of the two mansions, but persisted, nevertheless.*
>
> *To prove this, not long ago I went to Arlington with the person who told me the story. The room there used by the girls of those days does look toward Georgetown. There is a forest of tall trees there now, but trees can grow very tall in a hundred years.*

Marveling at the wondrous things the girls of Tudor Place experienced during their lifetimes, Ms. Ecker noted the news coverage of Britannia Peter's death on January 26, 1911, the day before she would have turned ninety-six. In an editorial headlined "A Long and Interesting Life," the *Baltimore Sun* reported:

> *Mrs. Britannia Wellington Kennon, who died at Tudor Place, her historic home in Georgetown, on the 26th instant, and who will be buried today, was for many years a most interesting figure in the social life of Washington. She was the last in her generation of the descendants of Mrs. Martha Washington. John Parke Custis, Mrs. Washington's son, left four children. One of his daughters, Martha, married Thomas Peter, and Mrs. Kennon was their daughter. She married Commodore Beverley Kennon, of the United States Navy, whose father was General Richard Kennon, of Washington's staff, a charter member of the Society of the Cincinnati, and a grandson of Sir William Skipwith. Commodore Kennon was killed in 1844 by the explosion on the U.S.S. Princeton, so Mrs. Kennon was a widow for more than sixty-six years.*
>
> *Tudor Place, Mrs. Kennon's home, was famous for the distinguished guests that were entertained there, among them being General Lafayette, who visited there in 1824. She was the center of an intellectual and cultivated society, and was always in touch with the progress of events in the world.*
>
> *Mrs. Kennon was born three weeks after the Battle of New Orleans, and several months before the Battle of Waterloo. Her life spanned the period of the great advance in the appliances of civilization in this and the last century.*

It was very important that the news of the battle of Waterloo should reach London without delay, and yet with every appliance and speed then known, it took three days for the news to reach England. Indeed, when Mrs. Kennon was thirty-two years of age, it required eight months to travel from New England to Oregon. At the age of fifteen she could have been a passenger on the first passenger railroad train that was ever run; until she was five years old, there was no such thing as an iron plow in all the world, and until she was grown up, the people were dependent on tinder boxes and sun glasses to light their fires.

She had reached the age of twenty-three years when steam communication between Europe and America was established, and when the first telegram ever sent passed between Baltimore and Washington she was still a young woman. If all the advances in civilization which took place during the lifetime of this remarkable lady were catalogued, they would make a singularly interesting list.[123]

George Washington spent his last night in Georgetown at Tudor Place, following an appearance at Georgetown College in 1798. News accounts noted that the former president traveled the several blocks from the campus to the Peter home on foot, with cheering townspeople lining the streets to catch a glimpse of him.

The citizens were ranged on either side while General Washington walked between them, uncovered and bowing to the people as he passed along. The Georgetown College boys were dressed in their uniforms consisting in part of blue coats and red waistcoats, and presented a fine appearance.[124]

Just down Q Street from Tudor Place, a cluster of row houses beginning at the corner of Thirtieth Street was called Cooke Row, home to financier Henry D. Cooke, the first territorial governor of the District of Columbia, who served two years before Alexander "Boss" Shepherd took over the job of rebuilding Washington after the Civil War. Cooke bought the property from the family of tobacco tycoon Francis Dodge. A number of fancy houses in the neighborhood belonged to members of the Dodge family, who operated a large wharf at the foot of Wisconsin Avenue and carried on extensive trade with the Caribbean.

"Each year there was a sale for buyers from large cities in the North on the Dodges' wharf," Ms. Ecker remembered.

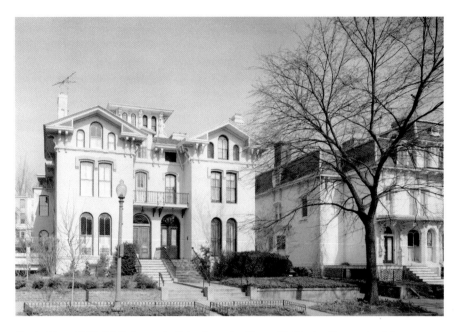

Cooke Row, 3007–29 Q Street, built by financier Henry D. Cooke, first territorial governor of the District of Columbia. Famous army physician Walter Reed lived in number 3021 of the complex. *Courtesy Library of Congress.*

> *It was quite an occasion. The counting house was capacious, and decorated with all sorts of curios from the tropics: sharks' jaws, flying fish, swordfish and sawfish; elaborate lunches were served to the patrons, with cigars and drinkables; chairs and benches were placed out on the platform overlooking the river. On summer afternoons, this was a great meeting place for the friends of the Dodges.*[125]

Governor Cooke owned many other Georgetown properties as well and was known for hosting grand balls attended by the leaders of Washington society, including his close friend President Ulysses Grant. Later, one of the row houses, number 3021, was the home of famous army physician Walter Reed.[126]

The largest and most palatial of the mansions adorning the Heights of Georgetown is Dumbarton Oaks, built on the highest point of Ninian Beall's Rock of Dumbarton estate. The land was purchased from Thomas Beall of George in 1800 by William H. Dorsey, the first judge of Georgetown's Orphan's Court, who was appointed by President Thomas Jefferson. Dorsey built the house, named it the Oaks and lived there for four years.

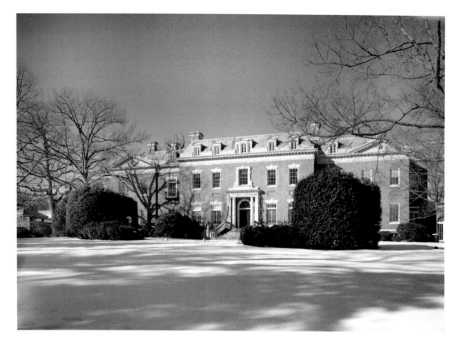

Dumbarton Oaks, at 3101 R Street, a palatial estate built by early tobacco barons. It was the former home of philanthropist Edward Magruder Linthicum and Vice President John C. Calhoun. The house, now part of Harvard University, was the site of a 1944 conference that helped establish the United Nations. *HABS (reproduction number HABS GEO, 234-1). Courtesy Library of Congress, Prints and Photographs Division.*

Later, it became the home of proslavery senator John C. Calhoun of South Carolina while he served as vice president under John Quincy Adams and Andrew Jackson, from 1825 until 1832. Calhoun also was secretary of war under President James Monroe and secretary of state under President John Tyler, in addition to serving in Congress. Calhoun once wrote that the "leisure of the office of Vice-President" allowed him time to study the "fundamentals of the American system" at the lofty home, which he called Acrolophos, meaning "grove on the hill." For a time, the house also was called Monterey after the famous battle of the Mexican War.

In 1846, the estate was bought by hardware merchant and philanthropist Edward Magruder Linthicum, who restored the former name of the Oaks and made the house and its extensive grounds "the show place of the District." In 1891, it was bought by Henry F. Blount, who had made a fortune manufacturing farm implements, and in 1920, it was purchased by Robert Woods Bliss, U.S. ambassador to Argentina. Bliss remodeled the house and gardens and renamed the estate Dumbarton Oaks. In 1940, he donated the property to Harvard University as a museum and center for the study of Byzantine art and culture. The center hosted the 1944 Dumbarton Oaks Conference, which led to the formation of the United Nations.[127]

Behind a high brick wall on the edge of Georgetown Heights, overlooking Rock Creek and the city of Washington, is a majestic residence called Evermay, built in 1801 by landowner Samuel Davidson. Davidson got rich selling real estate to the U.S. government, including land that became the north lawn of the White House and the adjacent Lafayette Park. His Federal-style brick home was designed by British architect Nicholas King, who helped Pierre L'Enfant design the city of Washington.

Davidson was one of early Georgetown's strangest characters. He intensely guarded his privacy and hired sentries to patrol the perimeter of Evermay to keep people out. He once placed an advertisement in local newspapers warning neighbors to stay away:

Evermay proclaims, take care, enter not here, for punishment is ever near.

Whereas, the height called Evermay, adjoining this town, is now completely enclosed with a good stone wall in part and a good post and rail fence thereto, this is to forewarn at their peril, all persons, of whatever age, color, or standing in society, from trespassing on the premises, in any manner, by day or by night; particularly all thieving knaves and idle vagabonds; all rambling parties; all assignation parties; all amorous bucks with their dorfies, and all sporting bucks with their dogs and guns.

My man, Edward, who resides on the premises, has my positive orders to protect the same from all trespassers as far as in his power, with the aid of the following implements, placed in his hands for that purpose, if necessary, viz: Law, when the party is worthy of that attention and proper testimony can be had, a good cudgel, tomahawk, cutlass, gun and blunderbuss, with powder, shot and bullets, steel traps and grass snakes. It is Edward's duty to obey my lawful commands. In so doing, on this occasion, I will defend him at all risques and hazards.

For the information of those persons who may have real business on the premises, there is a good and convenient gate. But mark! I do not admit mere curiosity an errand of business. Therefore, I beg and pray of all my neighbors to avoid Evermay as they would a den of devils, or rattle snakes, and thereby save themselves and me much vexation and trouble. June 2, 1810.—SAMUEL DAVIDSON.

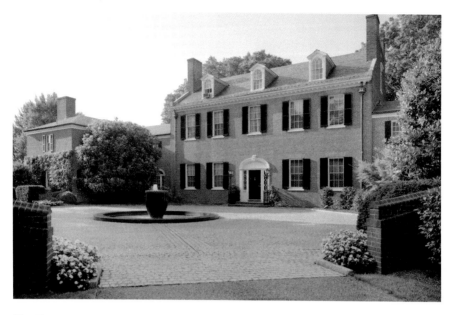

The Evermay estate, at 1623 Twenty-eighth Street, built in 1801 by Samuel Davidson with proceeds from his sale of land that became Lafayette Park and the north lawn of the White House. *Charles E. Peterson, 1942 (reproduction number HABS DC, GEO, 49-4). Courtesy Library of Congress, Prints and Photographs Division.*

Davidson is buried just outside the wall of Evermay in a portion of Oak Hill Cemetery that was once part of his estate.[128]

In the block across Twenty-eighth Street from Evermay is another historic homesite carved from Ninian Beall's Rock of Dumbarton. A granddaughter of the Beall family and her husband, wealthy planter Benjamin Mackall, built the estate called Mackall Square at 1623 Twenty-ninth Street. The Mackalls first constructed a frame house on the site, which was moved not far away to a spot just outside the gates of Tudor Place to make way for a larger brick home.[129]

Up the hill and around the corner at R and Thirtieth Streets is the former home of *Washington Post* publishers Philip and Katherine Graham, the scene of many of Georgetown's top social events for decades, until Mrs. Graham's death in 2001. Both are buried just across the street from the house, around the chapel of Oak Hill Cemetery.

Two houses built about 1840 at the corner of P and Twenty-eighth Streets are surrounded by a sturdy iron fence made of musket barrels salvaged from the Mexican War. The owner of the houses, Reuben Daw, was looking for an economical way to fence in his properties when he saw the old gun parts in a huge stack at a government surplus auction. Through the years, the property has been home to Admiral Charles Dwight Sigsbee, a Civil War veteran famous for commanding the USS *Maine* when it exploded in the harbor of Havana, Cuba, in 1898, killing 260 men. Former secretary of state Dean Acheson also lived there.

At the corner of Twenty-eighth and Q Streets (called Montgomery and Stoddert Streets in earlier days) stands a large home built in 1850 by Francis Dodge's son Robert, which is nearly identical to a nearby house built by his brother, Francis Dodge Jr. When first constructed, the home was known for its grandiose gardens, designed by landscape architect Andrew Jackson Downing, who also planned the grounds of the National Mall and the Capitol. Robert Dodge, a civil engineer who helped design the Aqueduct Bridge, also served as paymaster for the Union army during the Civil War and was noted for planting maple trees along the neighborhood streets. Later occupants included Warren Delano Robins, a cousin of President Franklin Roosevelt who served as ambassador to Canada, and lawyer and tennis champion Dwight Filley Davis, who competed at Wimbledon and in the 1904 Olympics. Davis—for whom the Davis Cup tennis trophy is named—also served as secretary of war under President Calvin Coolidge and as governor general of the Philippines under President Herbert Hoover.[130]

Near the Key Bridge on M Street is the embassy of Ukraine, which has a long and storied history in Georgetown. It was the home of General Uriah Forrest when he hosted the March 1791 dinner meeting at which George Washington made deals with local property owners to purchase land for the new capital city. Discussing the historic evening, Ms. Ecker mused:

> *What a scene that must have been! One can imagine the turtle soup, the fish and terrapin caught fresh from the river, wild ducks and ham with shoulders of mutton and all the vegetables and hot breads and other delectable foods for which Maryland is famous—for Uriah Forrest, himself a Marylander, had a Maryland wife, Rebecca Plater, the daughter of Governor Plater.*

After Forrest, who became mayor of Georgetown in 1792, moved elsewhere, the house was bought by William Marbury, who lost his renowned Supreme Court case against James Madison.[131]

Marbury's family kept the house for several generations. Marbury's grandson, also named William, was a Southern sympathizer during the

Civil War who, in the days following the Battle of Bull Run, famously bolted the doors and tightly shuttered the windows when "the damn Yankees" came streaming over the nearby bridge "at a dog-trot and dropped from exhaustion" on his front steps. Another legendary tale involved a young girl in the Marbury family taking a friend to Oak Hill Cemetary to place flowers on the grave of an infant daughter of Confederate President Jefferson Davis. Prior to the war, Davis had lived in Washington as a senator from Mississippi and as a secretary of war under President Franklin Pierce.

Authorities spotted the girls at the Rebel grave site and arrested them. Hearing that soldiers were on the way to search her house, Marbury's wife grabbed a stack of letters from her nephews in the Confederate army and hurriedly sewed them into a chair cushion. Years later, three of her great-grandchildren who inherited her furniture heard the story, spied an odd stitching job on one of the chairs, slit the cushion open and found the letters.[132]

On the southeast corner of Thirty-fourth and Prospect Streets stands the mansion once owned by tobacco exporter Benjamin Stoddert, a business partner of Uriah Forrest. Stoddert collaborated with George Washington in a scheme to purchase acreage along the Potomac prior to the announcement of the area's selection as the new U.S. capital. Stoddert bought the land before speculators could drive up the price and then turned it over to the government. Later, President John Adams appointed Stoddert to be the first secretary of the navy.

Stoddert called his home Halcyon House, and "what a suitable and lovely name for one in his business," Ms. Ecker opined,

> *for the halcyon was a fabled bird, whose nest floated upon the sea. It had the power of charming winds and waves, hence, "halcyon days" are days of tranquility and peace. From his southern dormer windows, tradition says, Major Stoddert used to watch with his telescope for the coming of some of those ships that he and Colonel Forrest and Colonel Murdock sent out across the ocean.*

But the tranquility and peace of Halcyon House apparently could be disrupted by Stoddert's children, as suggested in a letter that his wife, Rebecca, wrote to someone who had asked to visit the youngsters: "I wonder that you can be so anxious to see my children, for a parcel of rude, disagreeable brats as ever was born, except the two youngest."[133]

On the northeast corner of N and Thirty-fourth Streets (called First and Frederick before the street names changed) is a row of houses built

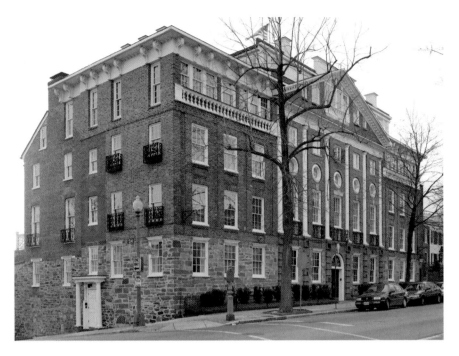

Halcyon House, at 3400 Prospect Street, home of shipper Benjamin Stoddert, who served in the Revolution and became one of Georgetown's wealthiest citizens. *Courtesy Library of Congress.*

by longtime mayor John Cox, who led city hall from 1822 to 1845. Cox, a colonel in the War of 1812, was a merchant and landowner known for his impeccable neatness and lavish parties. The house at number 3357 in the block known as "Cox's Row" was the site of his famous reception for Lafayette in 1824.[134]

The oldest brick house in Georgetown is believed to be number 3033 N Street, built by original landowner George Beall using money he received for turning over part of his Rock of Dumbarton estate to the City of Georgetown in 1751. Beall bequeathed the house to his daughter, Elizabeth, who married longtime Presbyterian leader Stephen Bloomer Balch.

A nearby house, at 3017 N Street, was built by Beall's son, Thomas Beall of George. Several noteworthy citizens have lived there, including Major George Peter, the youngest son of Georgetown's first mayor, Robert Peter, whose distinguished career included receiving his military commission from George Washington, helping organize the territorial government of Missouri, being part of a delegation that welcomed the Lewis and Clark expedition from its exploration of the West, testifying at the trial of former vice president Aaron Burr following his deadly duel with Alexander Hamilton, serving as an artillery officer in the War of 1812 and later serving in Congress.

In the late 1800s, when a family named Smoot owned the house, a repair crew discovered a mummified cat inside a basement wall, causing great excitement in the neighborhood. "The complete body of this feline, including a long, tenuous tail, was found standing on its four feet between two walls where it had been trapped evidently, years earlier," writer Josephine Davis Leary reported in her book *Backward Glances at Georgetown*. "Mrs. Smoot directed the workmen to take it carefully upstairs to the library for all to see, and it was on exhibition for quite a while. Stoney-gray, thin almost as paper, it was a strange sight long to be remembered."[135]

Other residents of number 3017 have included Newton Baker, secretary of war under President Woodrow Wilson, and former first lady Jacqueline Kennedy Onassis, who moved into the house after her husband's assassination in 1963. Prior to his election as president, John F. Kennedy and his wife lived in a house at 3307 N Street that once belonged to William Marbury.[136]

The N Street neighborhood also was the site of the original Beall family burying ground. About 1890, the graves were relocated to a larger cemetery. Resident Sally Somervell Mackall related a sometimes-disputed tale that "when the body of Ninian Beall was removed, his skeleton was found in perfect preservation, and measured six feet and seven inches, and his hair, which was very red, had retained its natural color." Two headstones in the old graveyard read: "Here lieth Colonel George Beall, who departed this life March 15, 1780, aged 85" and "Here lieth the body of Elizabeth Beall, who departed this life October 2, 1748, aged about 49 years."[137]

The house at 3014 N Street once belonged to Judge James Dunlop, a law partner of Francis Scott Key. Dunlop was serving as chief justice of the Circuit Court of the District of Columbia in 1861 when the Civil War began and President Lincoln fired him because of his Southern sympathies. Lincoln then offered the judgeship to attorney William Redin, who lived across the street, but Redin refused the appointment, telling Lincoln that he would not replace his old friend and neighbor. Interestingly, Judge Dunlop's heirs sold the house in 1915 to Lincoln's son, Robert Todd Lincoln, who lived there for several years. Lincoln served as secretary of war under Presidents James Garfield and Chester A. Arthur and as ambassador to Britain under President Benjamin Harrison. The garden of the house contains the last remaining stone marker used by surveyors in designating Georgetown's original boundaries in 1751.[138]

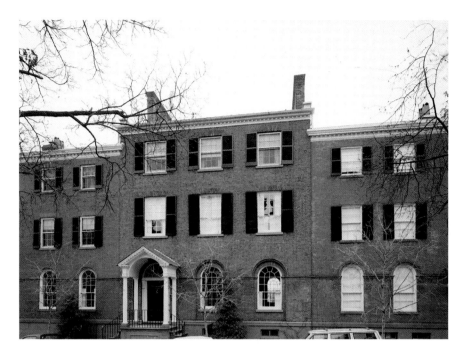

The Laird-Dunlop House, at 3014 N Street, was the former home of Judge James Dunlop, who was fired from the Circuit Court of the District of Columbia by President Lincoln because of his Southern sympathies when the Civil War broke out. Later, Lincoln's son, Robert Todd Lincoln, bought the house. *HABS (reproduction number HABS, GEO, 154-1). Courtesy Library of Congress, Prints and Photographs Division.*

One of the earliest integrated schools in America was founded in Georgetown by English immigrant Mary Billings in 1807. But the school was short-lived because of "a great deal of prejudice arising on the subject" of teaching "both colored and white children together." She then decided to focus on educating black children and opened the Billings School at 3100 Dumbarton Avenue, where she taught until her death in 1826.[139]

On March 27, 1935, folks living around Thirty-first and O Streets were surprised by a noisy parade that stopped at 3131 O Street to visit an old gentleman on his ninety-first birthday. The honoree was General Adolphus Greely, a Civil War veteran who also had taken part in one of the earliest expeditions to the North Pole. As a military band played "The Star-Spangled Banner," Supreme Court justice Owen J. Roberts delivered a special present—a long-delayed Congressional Medal of Honor commemorating General Greely's lifetime of distinguished service in the U.S. Army. In addition to the War Between the States, his military assignments included

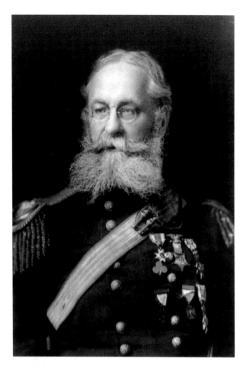

General Adolphus Greely (1844–1935), the Civil War veteran and explorer who was honored at his Georgetown home on his ninety-first birthday with a Congressional Medal of Honor for his long career of distinguished military service. *Bain News Service Company. Courtesy Library of Congress, George G. Bain Collection.*

the 1881–84 Signal Corps Meteorological Expedition to the Arctic and an assignment as chief signal officer in the Spanish-American War, when he oversaw communications operations in Puerto Rico, Cuba and the Philippines.[140]

One of the most visited buildings in Georgetown is also the oldest in the District of Columbia: the "Old Stone House" on M Street, whose owners through the years included tavern keeper John Suter Jr. The small blue-granite dwelling, rumored to have been L'Enfant's office when he planned the city of Washington in the 1790s, is now operated by the National Park Service as a museum depicting the simple life of colonial times amid the grandeur of the more affluent colonial families of old Georgetown.

Few neighborhoods in America can rival the rich history of Georgetown, and few are more revered by their residents or more popular with tourists "lured hither by the quiet dignity of the old-time atmosphere," according to Grace Dunlop Ecker, whose firsthand memories have made such a vivid contribution to the written records of "this dear old town of my birth where my parents, my grandparents, great-grandfathers and one great-great-grandfather lived, and which I love so dearly." When writing her book *A Portrait of Old George Town* in the early 1930s, Ms. Ecker opened with a poem by William Tipton Tablott, entitled "George Town Ghosts," to evoke the character of her hometown and its unique place in history:

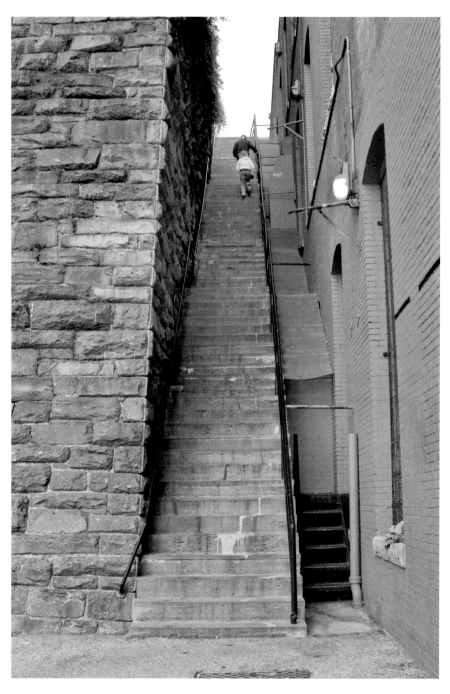

Tourists and local joggers troop up and down a long concrete staircase near the Georgetown University campus. The stairs gained fame in the 1970s, when they were featured in the classic horror movie *The Exorcist. Photo by Missy Loewe.*

The ghosts of Georgetown when they meet
In haunted house or moonlit street
With pride recall the functions gay
When down the Philadelphia way
The Federal City overnight
Moved to its bare and swampy site,
For Georgetown then a busy mart,
A growing seaport from the start,
Where a whole-hearted spirit reigned,
Threw wide its doors, and entertained
With wines and viands of the best—
The Federal City was its guest.

In memory of the good old days,
Whose ways to them were modern ways,
Congenial ghosts across Rock Creek,
With formal bows and steps antique,
Rehearse a spectral minuet
Where once in bright assemblies met—
Beruffled belles looked love to beaus
In powdered wigs and faultless hose;
Or merchant ghosts survey the skies
And venture guesses weather-wise
Regarding winds that will prevail
To speed their ships about to sail.

Still in the shaded hillside streets
A trace of old-time welcome greets
The passer-by who has a flare
For scenes of old. No longer there
A buoyant Georgetown stands alone,
The Federal City having grown
Until their boundaries overlap;
So that, deleted from the map,
Though once the Federal City's host,
Georgetown itself is now a ghost.[141]

Notes

CAPTAINS AND INDIANS
1. Ecker, *Portrait*, 7–9.
2. Evans, "Old Georgetown," 8–9.
3. Ibid., 9.
4. Froncek, *City of Washington*, 12.
5. Fausz, "Present at the 'Creation,'" 9–10.
6. Hawley and Lewger, *Relation of Maryland*, 72–73.
7. *Proceedings*, 7–20.

THE SCOTTISH STAKE THEIR CLAIM
8. Ecker, *Portrait*, 11.
9. Ibid., 12.

MONEY BY THE HOGSHEAD
10. Ibid.
11. Scharf, *History of Maryland*, 46.

THE GEORGES OF GEORGETOWN
12. Ecker, *Portrait*, 13.

TYCOONS AND TAVERNS
13. Ibid.
14. Ibid., 20–21.
15. Ibid., 21.
16. Ibid., 13.
17. Ibid., 15.
18. Lesko, Babb and Gibbs, *Black Georgetown*, 2.
19. Bryan, *History of the Capital*, 76.
20. Mackall, *Early Days*, 69.
21. Ecker, *Portrait*, 46.
22. Jackson, *Chronicles*, 75.

23. Mackall, *Early Days*, 44.
24. Jackson, *Chronicles*, 218; and Mackall, *Early Days*, 33.
25. Ecker, *Portrait*, 38.
26. Ibid.

THE CAPITAL ACROSS THE CREEK
27. Ibid.
28. Bryan, *History of the Capital*, 37.
29. Mackall, *Early Days*, 14.
30. Ecker, *Portrait*, 38.
31. Ibid., 39.
32. Ibid., 40.
33. Ibid., 41.
34. Ibid., 43.
35. Ibid., 48.

AMERICA'S FIRST SUBURB
36. Ibid., 44–45.
37. Ibid., 45.
38. Ibid., 24; and Froncek, *City of Washington*, 74.
39. Ecker, *Portrait*, 121.
40. Mackall, *Early Days*, 286–90.
41. Ibid.
42. Ecker, *Portrait*, 35.
43. Ibid.
44. Ibid., 35–36.
45. Ibid., 37.
46. Ibid., 36.
47. Jackson, *Chronicles*, 104.
48. Mackall, *Early Days*, 73–74.
49. Ecker, *Portrait*, 35–40.
50. Jackson, *Chronicles*, 245.
51. Ibid., 102.

OFF TO BATTLE, UP IN FLAMES
52. Ecker, *Portrait*, 48–49.
53. Ibid., 56–57.
54. Ibid., 156.
55. Ibid., 60–61.
56. Ibid., 134.
57. Ibid., 135.
58 Mackall, *Early Days*, 81; and Ecker, *Portrait*, 57.

PLAGUES OF PROGRESS
59. Jackson, *Chronicles*, 120–24.
60. Ibid., 118.
61. Ibid., 105.
62. Ibid., 104–05.
63. Ecker, *Portrait*, 51; and Froncek, *City of Washington*, 146.
64. Jackson, *Chronicles*, 40–42.
65. Ibid., 69–78.
66. Ibid., 62–63.

High Society
67. Ecker, *Portrait*, 135–36.
68. Ibid., 50.
69. Ibid., 59.
70. Mackall, *Early Days*, 301–08.
71. Ecker, *Portrait*, 32.
72. Leary, *Backward Glances*, 13–14.
73. Ecker, *Portrait*, 33.
74. Froncek, *City of Washington*, 91.
75. Ecker, *Portrait*, 32.
76. Mackall, *Early Days*, 316–22.
77. Ecker, *Portrait*, 96–97.
78. Ibid., 90–97.
79. Ibid., 92.
80 Ibid, 4.

For Sale: Family of Five
81. Lesko, Babb and Gibbs, *Black Georgetown*, 2.
82. Froncek, *City of Washington*, 168–73.
83. Ibid., 170–71.
84. Paynter, "Fugitives of the *Pearl*," 243–64.
85. Ecker, *Portrait*, 68.
86. Froncek, *City of Washington*, 212.
87. Ibid., 202–12.
88. Ibid., 203.
89. Ecker, *Portrait*, 101–02.
90. Froncek, *City of Washington*, 212.
91. Lesko, Babb and Gibbs, *Black Georgetown*, 19.
92. Froncek, *City of Washington*, 222.
93. Ecker, *Portrait*, 144.
94. Ibid., 75–76.

Who Moved My Street?
95. Jackson, *Chronicles*, 74–75.
96. Ibid., 65–66.
97. Ibid., 333.
98. Ibid., 53–56.
99. Leary, *Backward Glances*, 19–20.
100. Ecker, *Portrait*, 86.
101. Ibid., 128.
102. Ibid., 111.
103. Ibid., 150–51.

Preaching, Teaching and Pulling Teeth
104. Jackson, *Chronicles*, 143.
105. Mackall, *Early Days*, 112–13.
106. Jackson, *Chronicles*, 152–62.
107. Ibid., 186–88.
108. Ibid., 204–05.
109. Ibid., 209.
110. Ibid., 214.
111. Ecker, *Portrait*, 68.
112. Jackson, *Chronicles*, 215–16.

113. Ibid., 228.
114. Ecker, *Portrait*, 68–69.
115. Jackson, *Chronicles*, 228–29.
116. Ibid., 238–44.
117. Ecker, *Portrait*, 89.
118. Jackson, *Chronicles*, 238–44.
119. Leary, *Backward Glances*, 9–10; and Froncek, *City of Washington*, 138.
120. Jackson, *Chronicles*, 251–65.
121. Ibid., 252.

Ghost Town
122. Ecker, *Portrait*, 131–33.
123. Ibid., 134–39.
124. Froncek, *City of Washington*, 74.
125. Ecker, *Portrait*, 126.
126. Carrier, *Historic Georgetown*, 109.
127. Whitehill, *Dumbarton Oaks*, 38–70.
128. Ecker, *Portrait*, 144–145; and Mackall, *Early Days*, 309.
129. Ecker, *Portrait*, 146–47.
130. Ibid., 130–31; and Carrier, *Historic Georgetown*, 102.
131. Ecker, *Portrait*, 58.
132. Ibid., 60.
133. Ibid., 65–66.
134. Ibid., 71–72.
135. Leary, *Backward Glances*, 29–30.
136. Carrier, *Historic Georgetown*, 54, 129.
137. Mackall, *Early Days*, 48.
138. Ecker, *Portrait*, 80–85.
139. Carrier, *Historic Georgetown*, 117; and Ecker, *Portrait*, 106.
140. Ecker, *Portrait*, 112.
141. Ibid., 2–4.

BIBLIOGRAPHY

Adams, Abigail. *Letters of Mrs. Adams, the Wife of John Adams*. Boston: Charles C. Little and James Brown, 1840.

Arber, Edward. *Travels and Works of Captain John Smith*. Edinburgh: Kessinger Publishers LLC, 1910.

Barnett, Todd H. "Tobacco, Planters, Tenants and Slaves: A Portrait of Montgomery County in 1783." *Maryland Historical Magazine* (1994).

Brown, Letitia Woods. *Free Negroes in the District of Columbia, 1790–1846*. New York: Oxford University Press, 1972.

Bryan, Wilhelmus Bogart. *A History of the National Capital; from Its Foundation through the Period of the Adoption of the Organic Act*. Vol. 1, 1790–1814. New York: Macmillan Co., 1914.

Caemmerer, H. Paul. *The Life of Pierre Charles L'Enfant, Planner of the City Beautiful, the City of Washington*. Washington, D.C.: National Republic Publishing Co., 1950.

Carrier, Thomas J. *Historic Georgetown: A Walking Tour*. Charleston, SC: Arcadia Publishing, 1999.

Curran, Robert Emmett. *The Bicentennial History of Georgetown University: From Academy to University 1789–1889*. Washington, D.C.: Georgetown University Press, 1993.

Ecker, Grace Dunlop. *A Portrait of Old George Town*. N.p.: Garrett & Massie Inc., 1933. Reprint, Richmond, VA: Dietz Press Inc., 1951.

Ellis, John B. *The Sights and Secrets of the National Capital: A Work Descriptive of Washington City in All Its Various Phases*. New York: United States Publishing Co., 1869.

Evans, Henry Ridgley. "Old Georgetown on the Potomac." *Georgetown News*, 1933.

Fausz, J. Frederick. "Present at the 'Creation': The Chesapeake World that Greeted the Maryland Colonists." *Maryland Historical Magazine* 79 (Spring 1984): 9–10.

Froncek, Thomas, ed. *The City of Washington: An Illustrated History*. Avenel, NJ: Junior League of Washington, Wings Books, 1977.

Gutheim, Frederick Albert, and Antoinette J. Lee. *Worthy of a Nation: Washington, D.C., from L'Enfant to the National Capital*. Baltimore, MD: Johns Hopkins University Press, 2006.

Hawley, Jerome, and John Lewger. *A Relation of Maryland, 1666, Narratives of Early Maryland, 1633–1684*. New York: Charles Scribner's Sons, 1910.

BIBLIOGRAPHY

Idzerda, Stanley J., Anne C. Loveland and Marc H. Miller. *Lafayette, Hero of Two Worlds: The Art and Pageantry of His Farewell Tour of America, 1824–1825*. Flushing, NY: The Queens Museum, 1989.

Jackson, Richard Plummer. *The Chronicles of Georgetown, D.C., from 1751 to 1878*. Washington, D.C.: R.O. Polkinhorn, Printer, 1878.

King, Leroy O. *100 Years of Capital Traction: The Story of Streetcars in the Nation's Capital*. Dallas, TX: Taylor Publishing Co., 1989.

Leary, Josephine Davis. *Backward Glances at Georgetown*. Richmond, VA: Dietz Press Inc., 1947.

Lesko, Kathleen M., Valevia Melissa Babb and Carroll R. Gibbs. *Black Georgetown Remembered*. Washington, D.C.: Georgetown University Press, 1991.

Mackall, Sally Somervell. *Early Days of Washington*. Washington, D.C.: Neale Co., 1899. Reprint, Sterling, IL: G.E. Bishop Printing Co., 1934.

Marck, John T. *Maryland—The Seventh State: A History*. Glen Arm, MD: Creative Impressions Ltd., 1995.

McCoy, Jerry A. "The Baron Bodisco House." *Georgetowner*, February 19, 2004.

Mitchell, Mary J. *Glimpses of Georgetown: Past and Present*. Washington, D.C.: Road Street Press, 1983.

Mitchell, Pauline A. "Gaskins, Mt. Zion United Methodist Church—History." Mt. Zion United Methodist Church. www.coax.net/people/lwf.

Paynter, John. "The Fugitives of the *Pearl*." *Journal of Negro History* (July 1916): 243–64.

Proceedings of the General Assembly. Vol. 3. Archives of Maryland, February 28, 1637.

Proctor, John Clagett, ed. *Washington Past and Present*. New York: Lewis Historical Publishing Co., 1930.

Scharf, J. Thomas. *History of Maryland: From the Earliest Periods to the Present Day*. Hartsboro, PA: Tradition Press, 1967.

Whitehill, Walter Muir. *Dumbarton Oaks: The History of a Georgetown House and Garden, 1800–1966*. Cambridge, MA: Belknap Pres of Harvard University Press, 1967.

INDEX

ABOUT THE AUTHORS

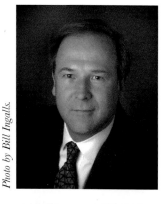

Photo by Bill Ingalls.

David Mould, a public relations executive and journalist, has managed communications for Fortune 500 companies and the U.S. space program. In addition to writing about history, he has been a reporter and editor at major newspapers and United Press International. He lives in Washington, D.C., with his wife, Lisa, and children, David and Lesley.

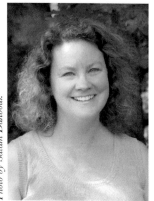

Photo by Salam Dahbour.

Missy Loewe is the academic dean at the Washington School of Photography and sits on the board of directors for many arts and historic preservation groups. Originally from Spokane, Washington, Missy has spent the last twenty-five years as a D.C.-area resident. She and her husband live with a border collie and three cats (which get herded a lot) in Gaithersburg, Maryland.